Twitter

DUMMIES®

POCKET EDITION

**by Laura Fitton, Michael E. Gruen,
and Leslie Poston**

WILEY

John Wiley & Sons, Inc.

Twitter® For Dummies®, Pocket Edition

Published by
John Wiley & Sons, Inc.
111 River Street
Hoboken, NJ 07030-5774
www.wiley.com

WILEY

Publisher's Acknowledgments

We're proud of this book; please send us your comments through our online registration form located at http://dummies.custhelp.com. For other comments, please contact our Customer Care Department within the U.S. at 877-762-2974, outside the U.S. at 317-572-3993, or fax 317-572-4002.

Some of the people who helped bring this book to market include the following:

Acquisitions and Editorial

Project Editor: Kevin Kirschner

Executive Editor: Steve Hayes

Copy Editor: Teresa Artman

Technical Editor: Zachary Szukala

Sr. Editorial Assistant:
Cherie Case

Cartoons: Rich Tennant
(www.the5thwave.com)

Composition Services

Project Coordinator: Kristie Rees

Layout and Graphics:
Andrea Hornberger,
Kathie Rickard,
Lavonne Roberts

Proofreader: Dwight Ramsey

Publishing and Editorial for Technology Dummies

Richard Swadley, Vice President and Executive Group Publisher

Andy Cummings, Vice President and Publisher

Mary Bednarek, Executive Acquisitions Director

Mary C. Corder, Editorial Director

Publishing for Consumer Dummies

Kathleen Nebenhaus, Vice President and Executive Publisher

Composition Services

Debbie Stailey, Director of Composition Services

Table of Contents

• •

Introduction

• •

*H*ave you heard? All the world's a-twitter!

Twitter is a tool that you can use to send and receive short, 140-character messages from your friends, organizations you care about, businesses you frequent, publications you read, or complete strangers who share (or not) your interests.

As a user of Twitter, you choose whose updates you want to receive — which people you want to follow. In turn, other users can elect to follow your updates. You can send messages publicly for the entire Twitter community, semi-publicly to users whom you approve to receive your messages, or privately from one user to another. You can view these messages — called *tweets* (sometimes called *updates*) — on the Internet or on your cellphone.

Twitter has changed and enhanced how people can communicate with each other, with brands and companies, and with social movements and initiatives. Twitter has empowered users to raise money for people in need, coordinate rescue efforts in the wake of a natural disaster, and alert authorities to emergencies and illegal activities both domestic and abroad.

Skeptical of what you can say in 140 characters? The first paragraph of the Introduction weighs in at 42 characters. This paragraph? 137.

You may also find, over time, that you communicate more effectively and that your writing becomes shorter and more to the point. You can say a lot within very little space; and because it takes only a little time to read and update, you may be surprised about how much value you, your friends, and your family can extract from Twitter.

About This Book

We, the authors (Laura, Michael, and Leslie), aren't employees, representatives, or shareholders in Twitter. The opinions that we give in this book represent what's worked for us and our networks, but not necessarily the Twitter world at large. We've been on Twitter for quite a while, and we have a good sense about how people are using it. But Twitter is a living, breathing, and constantly changing dynamic community. Much of Twitter's value comes from the ecosystem of tools built by others to work together with Twitter. Hundreds of these new tools launch every month. Twitter itself may change its feature set, its privacy features, or general direction overnight, which changes how people use it.

Twitter has released a number of enhancements to its interface that make it even easier and more accessible to interact with the community. Although the layout and the exact location of everything may change around a bit, the basics of Twitter likely will always be the same. After you understand how the service works, you can pretty easily find any feature that may have moved since the publication of this book. You can also keep up with the *Twitter For Dummies* community through the #dummies hashtag (if you're up-to-date on hashtags).

New for Pocket Edition

This Pocket Edition shows updated screenshots and how-to's to reflect the latest changes in the Twitter. com interface. (Screenshots in this book show you what the interface was like in spring 2012.) However, remember that Twitter is an Internet product and is subject to change at any time, so please use this book as a guide, not the be-all and end-all of the Twitter experience.

Lastly, the *Twitter For Dummies,* Pocket Edition, author team has had a few changes: Leslie, previously known as @geechee_girl, is now known as @leslie. Laura still goes by @pistachio, and is the Founder and CEO of oneforty (or @oneforty on Twitter). Michael now protects his tweets out of suppressed teenage rebellion and for no otherwise discernible reason.

Foolish Assumptions

In this book, we make the following assumptions:

- ✔ You're at least 13 years of age. (You have to be at least 13 years old to have a Twitter account.)

- ✔ You have access to a computer and the Internet (and know how to use them).

- ✔ You have a working e-mail address that you can access.

- ✔ You have a mobile phone and know how to send text messages (if you want to access Twitter by using your mobile phone).

- ✔ *Bonus:* You have a smartphone (if you want to use a mobile Twitter application).

- ✔ You can read.

Icons Used in This Book

Icons in this book point out important tidbits for you to look at, remember, and absorb. In this section, we go over the icons that we use throughout the book to guide you on your Twitter journey.

 The Tip icon points out helpful information that's likely to improve your Twitter experience.

 The Remember icon marks interesting or useful facts that we cover in detail in earlier chapters or something that's so important that you need to remember it while you're using Twitter.

 The Privacy icon denotes that you should be careful about the Twitter activities that we're discussing. You may find yourself with a security or privacy concern.

 The Warning icon highlights potential danger. When we use this icon, we're letting you know that you should proceed with caution.

 Whenever you see this icon, rest assured that we're letting our inner geeks run wild. Here we point out information that's interesting but not absolutely necessary to your understanding of the topic at hand. If you want all the details you can get, read these paragraphs. If you just want to know the basics, skip it.

Chapter 1

Hello, Twitter World

- -

In This Chapter
▶ Understanding what Twitter's all about
▶ Getting your Twitter party started
▶ Coming up with a good Twitter name
▶ Mixing it up: Making friends and saying hi

- -

*Y*ou may have heard of Twitter but have no idea what it actually is. Twitter is basically a powerful *mobile* social network that allows you to keep up with the people, businesses, and organizations you're interested in — whether you know them personally or not. It also lets you share what you're doing with the world — everyone from your family and friends to complete strangers. (You'll have to bear with us to find out why you would want to do that.) Harvard Professor Andrew McAfee (@amcafee) describes Twitter this way: "With Twitter, my friends are never far away."

Every day, we see dozens of new ideas and ways to use Twitter. In this chapter, we do our best to introduce the basic ideas and explain how Twitter works and why it's so powerful.

Figuring Out This Twitter Thing

Twitter is a powerful way to exchange ideas and information, and to stay in touch with people, businesses, and organizations that you care about. It's a social network — a digital abstraction that represents who you know and who you're interested in, regardless of whether you actually know them — that you can access from your computer, your cellphone, or any device with an Internet connection.

Twitter has one hallmark quirk: You can instantly post entries of only 140 characters or less — *tweets*. Your tweets are managed through the www. twitter.com site or your cellphone, or by way of the numerous applications that are available for both.

On the most basic level, Twitter is a communications network that combines elements of Short Message Service (SMS or *texting*); instant messaging (IM) communication tools, such as AOL Instant Messenger (AIM); and blog publishing software, such as Blogger or WordPress. Like blogging, your tweets are generally published to the world at large where anyone can read them on Twitter.com (unless you choose a private account, so that only those you choose can see your tweets). Unlike blogging, though, you're limited to just 140 characters. And even like IM, you can communicate directly with people (through direct messages), but each Twitter message has its own uniform resource locator (URL), so each message is actually a web page. IM also lacks the social network "following" features of Twitter and basic ideas like "publish-subscribe" and one-to-many broadcasting of messages. Think you can't say anything meaningful in 140 characters? Think again. Twitterers innovate clever forms of one-liners, haiku, quotes, stories, and humor. Too, tweets can use links — in 23 percent of all tweets, by one measure — and links lead to a lot more information and context. Writing 140-character messages might seem limiting, and professional copy-writers will attest that writing succicnt headlines and tight advertising copy is hard to do really well. They will also tell you, though, that the right words can be quite powerful. Consider the impact of a gem like this: "Man Lands on Moon."

The idea of Twitter sounds simple, and it is: decep-tively simple. When you think about how millions of people around the world post Twitter messages, follow other people's Twitter streams, and respond to one another, you can start to see the significance behind Twitter's appeal. In fact, Twitter has noticed that it acts like a "pulse of the planet," a *zeitgeist* of what everyone is thinking about and doing and feel-ing, right now. Now that's pretty interesting!

True, Twitter can look like it's full of noise. But, after you find interesting people and accounts to follow, your Twitter stream shifts from a cascade of dis-jointed chatter to one of the most versatile, useful online communications tools yet seen — that is, if you take the time to learn to use that tool correctly.

Twitter is a great way for you or your company to connect with large numbers of people quickly and personally, just like you were having a con-versation. In tech-speak, Twitter is a microblog-ging or microsharing tool; however, you can more easily think of Twitter as a giant cocktail party with dozens of conversations you can join (or start) at any moment. Or, if you prefer a work metaphor, Twitter is like the office water cooler, where any number of informal (or formal) conversations can take place.

If you're familiar with blogs, IM, and web-based jour-nals, you can start to understand what makes Twitter unique. The web offers a lot of information. Twitter can turn those long articles, lengthy conversations, and far-reaching connections into easily digestible facts, thoughts, questions, ideas, concepts, and sound bites. In other words, when you have only 140 characters, you're forced to be succinct.

Signing Up

For many web services, signing up is the easiest part of an otherwise complicated process. With Twitter, using the site is just as easy as signing up.

To sign up for a Twitter account, follow these steps:

1. **Use your web browser to navigate to the Twitter website at http://twitter.com.**

   The Twitter splash page appears, as shown in Figure 1-1.

Figure 1-1: The Twitter sign-in page.

2. **Click the large Sign Up for Twitter button.**

   The signup page appears, as shown in Figure 1-2.

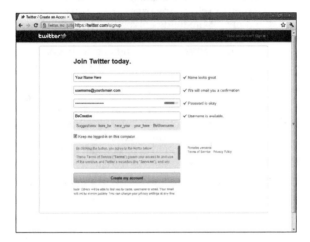

Figure 1-2: The very short and simple Twitter signup page.

3. **Type your basic information and desired user-name in the appropriate text boxes.**

   The only information Twitter requires from you is a name, a unique e-mail address where Twitter can contact you for notifications, a password of your choice, and a username. (You'll probably take longer to decide on a username than to actually sign up. We cover how to choose a good Twitter name in the following section.)

    Later, select the check box of the inbox of the e-mail account you enter in this step to confirm your Twitter account. Click the embedded link in the e-mail Twitter sends you to activate your account.

4. **Click the Create My Account button.**

   Twitter may immediately accept your information and create your account or send you to a CAPTCHA screen or refresh the page in case you didn't fill out any of the fields correctly. Those will be indicated with a red marker. (In most cases, it's because you're trying to sign up with a user account that's already taken, or you mistyped your e-mail address.)

   By clicking the Create My Account button, you're agreeing to Twitter's Terms of Service. You see a link at the bottom of the page where you can read those Terms of Service if you like, or you can go to http://twitter.com/tos to read them.

5. **If necessary, type the CAPTCHA code in the Type the Words Above text box.**

   This step is a standard web tactic to prove that you're a human and not a spam program (see Figure 1-3).

Figure 1-3: Are you human?

6. **Twitter introduces itself with a simple page. Click the Next button to continue (see Figure 1-4).**

Figure 1-4: Trust us; it gets more exciting than this!

7. **Follow the onscreen tutorial to find people you want to follow.**

   To jump-start your Twitter experience, the sign-up process includes a way for you to find people you might want to follow based on category, and to automatically connect with people you know.

a. *Initially, look at the list of suggestions. Click the Follow button beside a Twitter account shown in the list to follow that person (see Figure 1-5).*

b. *If you like, type in a name or keyword into the search box on the left side of the screen to personalize the list.*

c. *Click the Next button.*

   You have the option of skipping steps (click the Skip This Step link) until you get to the main Twitter screen.

Figure 1-5: Looking for people to follow.

8. **Browse categories to find people to follow based on things you're interested in (see Figure 1-6).**

   Choose from several categories that range from News to Sports, Entertainment, Music, and so forth. Spend as much time as you like looking for interesting accounts to follow.

   You're prompted to follow five, but you can click Next to continue even if you follow only one, or choose to skip this step entirely.

9. **Import contacts from an e-mail account.**

   In this step, you have the option of searching for and importing contacts from your address book.

   Look at the list of services (see Figure 1-7) and click Search contacts beside a service that you have an account with.

Figure 1-6: Find people to follow based on your interests.

Figure 1-7: Search contacts and import accounts.

10. Upload a photo and write a short bio (see Figure 1-8).

This is the last major step. Click Upload Image to transfer a profile picture (affectionately called an "avvy," which is short for *avatar*) from your computer to your Twitter account.

Square pics work best, which means you may need to have a computer nerd edit yours for you. Make sure it's smaller than 700 kilobytes and is in the JPG, GIF, or PNG format.

If you want to skip this step, you can return and make these changes later. Just hit the Settings page and edit your Profile.

Figure 1-8: Getting to know you.

11. When finished, click Save.

You're taken to your newly created Twitter account (see Figure 1-9).

Figure 1-9: Welcome to Twitter!

 Did you know you can register for Twitter entirely by text from any cellphone? Get a friend started while you're away from a computer — you can create a new Twitter account from any cellphone at any time. Just send an SMS text message with the word "start" to 40404 (this is an example of Twitter shortcode) and follow the directions that are texted back to you to choose a username. Later, go to Twitter.com and look for the button labeled Already Using Twitter via SMS? Activate Your Account.

 If you already have a Twitter account, *do not* text "start" to 40404 or you will associate your phone number with a separate new account. You will not be able to add your phone to your original account until you remove your number from the new account you inadvertently

created. See upcoming instructions on how to
set up your phone to work with your existing
Twitter account.

Picking a Name

On Twitter, your username is your identity. Laura's
Twitter name, or *handle,* is @Pistachio, and it has
become the way that many people know her. She's
met thousands of people in real life after initially connecting with them through Twitter, and it's not
unusual for her to hear, "Hey, Pistachio!" from across
the street or across the room at a party. @Pistachio
has, in effect, become her nickname. If you want a
quick glimpse at the search engine "optimization"
(SEO) value of Twitter, just run a Google search for
the word pistachio and you'll find her Twitter account
is one of the very first search results. Crazy.

When we refer to Twitter usernames in this
book, we follow the convention of putting an at
sign (@) before the name because that's how
you refer to other users on Twitter. (For example, if you want to say that you're reading
Laura's book, you might say, "Reading @
Pistachio's book." That way, people who
follow you on Twitter can easily click over to
Laura's Twitter profile, in case they want to
follow her, too!) But when you're actually choosing a username, the @ isn't part of it. The only
characters you can use are uppercase and low-
ercase letters, and the underscore character (_).

That story emphasizes that you should think about
how you want to be perceived both on and off Twitter
and how your username fits into that perception.
Twitter is a far-reaching service, and if you get really

involved in the culture of Twitter, like the rest of the social web, it undoubtedly spills over into real life. The days of choosing anonymous handles such as soldierboy44, like you may have when you used IM programs or chat rooms in years past, are (for many) long gone.

We recommend signing up for Twitter by using your name or a variation of it as your username (assuming somebody else isn't already using it). It makes your experience with Twitter much easier when the line between online and offline blurs.

For example, if your name is John Ira, you may want to pick a Twitter username such as @johnira or @john. If users have already claimed those monikers, try adding an adjective or descriptor, such as @handsomejohn or @johntheterrible. If you prefer for people not to know who you are, you can choose a name that's a bit more generic. You can also use a handle that you've established on other websites. You may also want your username to match your e-mail address; for example, if your e-mail address is doglover1980@example.com, you may decide to use @doglover1980 as your Twitter name.

If you choose to use your last name only — say, Michael (@gruen) — you may find that no one can remember your first name.

Using Twitter for your business? You can use your company or business name as your username, and you can fill in that business name in the Name text box on the Settings page for your account. But if you do, be sure to include the names of anyone who handles the company Twitter account in the 160-character Bio text box on the Settings page (under Profile) for your Twitter profile.

If you're looking to be a bit more removed and really would prefer to use a nickname rather than your name, or your company or product name, choose a username that's friendly and accessible to the people you want to interact with. On Twitter, you want people to respond to you, not be put off by a risqué or otherwise questionable handle. (If you want to be risqué, go for it, but understand that you'll limit the other users who will be willing to interact with you.) Likewise, if you run into your Twitter pals at networking events or other real-life social situations, you want to make sure that you don't mind having your username written on your nametag or shouted out in greeting.

Lean toward using a short Twitter username. Tweets are only 140 characters, so when people reply, you leave them less room for message content if you have a longer name. Twitter limits your username to just 15 characters for this very reason. (For more on how to reply to another person on Twitter, turn to Chapter 2.)

Your Twitter name has power and influence on search engine optimization (SEO), or how close to the top of a search results list you appear in a search engine such as Yahoo! or Google. Businesses should consider using valuable keywords as their Twitter names.

Finding Contacts

When you first sign up for Twitter, you're prompted to see whether your friends are on Twitter (see Figure 1-10). Finding contacts on Twitter can be a lot of fun! The easiest way to find your friends is to import your friends and contacts from other services that you already use (such as Gmail, Yahoo! Mail, AOL, and

Hotmail). You may be pleasantly surprised at how many people you know who are already busy tweeting away.

Figure 1-10: See whether your friends are on Twitter by importing your e-mail address book.

To import contacts and make them part of your Twitter world during the registration process, follow these steps:

1. **Click #Discover (top left of the screen).**

2. **Select the Find Friends link.**

3. **Click Search Contacts beside the e-mail account type from which you want to import (left side of the screen).**

4. **Type your e-mail credentials (username and password) in the Your Email and Email Password text boxes in the pop-up window and sign in.**

Having Twitter automatically find your contacts involves entering your e-mail account password. Although Twitter has established itself as a trustworthy service, in general, be very cautious about sites that ask you for your e-mail address and password.

5. **Click the Authorize Access button.**

You have to agree to give Twitter access to the account you have chosen. Twitter then looks at your contact list from your e-mail account and gives you a list of all the people from your address book who are already on Twitter or that you may want to invite to join you.

6. **Select the people you want to follow.**

If you click the Follow All button, everyone in your address book who is on Twitter will be automatically followed for you. If you want to follow only some people in your address book, click the Follow button for each person.

When you follow people on Twitter, you see their updates on your Twitter home screen.

7. **When you finish selecting people to follow, click the Twitter logo at the upper left of the screen.**

Alternatively, if you didn't find all the people in your address book that you wanted to follow, you can invite them by using the Invite by Email tab along the page navigation. (For more on inviting people to join Twitter, see "Inviting Contacts," later in this chapter.)

If you're not careful about where you click, you can accidentally send an e-mail to everyone in your address book. However, if you want to invite all your contacts to join you on Twitter, go ahead and share the Twitter love!

8. **Repeat these steps for all your other e-mail net-works, if you have them.**

If you skip this step during the registration process, you can always search for people by first name, last name, or e-mail address by clicking the Discover link at the top of any Twitter page.

Using useful people-finding tools

Jumping into random conversations is a great way to find like-minded Twitter users, but it's not the only way. You can use a few tools to discover people on Twitter who share your interests or live near you.

One of the more interesting tools out there, TwitterLocal (www.twitterlocal.net), helps you find Twitter users by geographic location. It's a great way for people interested in real-life meet-ups, as well as those in localized industries (such as real estate and car sales) who use Twitter to drum up business, to contact each other.

Twellow (www.twellow.com) is another handy tool for widening the scope of your Twitter universe (which, yes, some call a *twitterverse*). Twellow sorts Twitter users by categories based on keywords found in the Bio sections of their profiles. Users can also claim Twellow profiles for any Twitter usernames that belong to them, by proving who they are. Claiming lets you edit the entry to add more categories or remove incorrect categories. Twellow is searchable by name, location, or category, similar to an online yellow pages for Twitter (hence the name "Twellow").

Searching by using Twitter Search

Twitter also has its own search engine — Twitter Search — which you can access by typing something in the Search field at the top of any Twitter page or by going to http://search.twitter.com. Just enter any keyword choice into the Twitter Search text box and then click the Search button, and Twitter not only brings you results in chronological order (with the most recent at the top), but also lets you know when people have made new tweets that match your search criteria and gives you the option to refresh the search results page.

You can use Twitter Search to find new people on Twitter by typing keywords connected to your interests or profession in the text box. Bonus: Because Twitter Search sorts results based on how recent they are, the people you discover through this search are likely very active Twitter users.

Twitter Search was originally built by another web startup called Summize, which had earned special privilege and access to Twitter's application program interface (API) to create a search engine for the microsharing service. Although Twitter officially acquired Summize and has since renamed it Twitter Search, Summize is still known to many (and affectionately referred to) by its original name.

To some Twitter users, an account that's following 500 people with only one or two people following it back is a warning sign that it may be a spam account — and you don't want people to think that you're a spammer. So take a relaxed approach, following a few people at a time, talking to them, and giving them time to follow you back before increasing your follower circle. Over time, your numbers swell on their own just because you're building a network and interacting with it.

Twitter users are often interested in meeting and talking with new people and want to hear fresh voices. If you talk about your passions, interact with people in and out of your network, and are genuine, you'll have no trouble finding people to follow and getting them to follow you back.

If you have a blog or website, create a friendly "Hello, Twitter people!" Twitter landing page that introduces yourself to people you follow or who may want to follow you, and link to that page on your Twitter profile so that it directly welcomes curious new people. Companies that tweet should definitely mention it on their own website so that it is clear whether their account is authentic. Todd Defren of SHIFT Communications (@tdefren) has pointed out that it's a particularly good idea for businesses to use a Twitter landing page to explain how they are using Twitter and offer ways to opt-out of any connections or communications.

Inviting Contacts

During the registration process, after you import your contacts from your e-mail address book, you have the option to invite any of your contacts who aren't yet using Twitter.

The process is really simple:

1. **On the Find Friends screen (see Figure 1-11), paste or type the e-mail addresses of each person you'd like to follow in the box.**

2. **Click the Invite Friends button.**

   An invitation to join Twitter will be sent to the people you select, letting them know that you're on Twitter and they can follow your updates by signing up for Twitter themselves. (If you're concerned, Twitter allows you to preview that e-mail if you click that link at the top of this page.)

Figure 1-11: Ask your friends to join the party!

If you haven't found friends who you know are on Twitter, you can search for them by following these steps:

1. **On the top navigation bar of any Twitter page, click the #Discover link.**

   The tabbed navigation loads below the navigation bar.

2. **Click Find Friends.**

3. **Enter the name or screen name of the person or company you're looking for in the search box.**

If you're looking for Conan O'Brien, you might just try searching for Conan, or use both names.

4. **After you enter all the names you want, click the Follow button.**

   You can't miss the Follow button. Each name that is listed has one to the right, as shown in Figure 1-12.

Figure 1-12: Follow people by searching for them.

If you don't opt to invite people during the registration process, or you want to invite people down the road, you can always e-mail people you know whom you think would most enjoy or benefit from Twitter, sending them a link to your Twitter profile and writing a note explaining what Twitter is. Many people choose this approach when they first join Twitter so that they can keep the invitation process personal.

Many Twitter users put Twitter handles on business cards and in e-mail signature lines. These actions are indirect invitations for the people who meet us in real life or interact with us in business to connect with us on Twitter, as well. The more people who join you on Twitter, the more effective your network becomes.

Tweeting Like a Pro

Simply put, a *tweet* is what you call the 140-character message that you send out onto the web by using Twitter.

Why call it a tweet? It's convenient, tying into the whole theme of birds chirping. Also, like much of the Twitter vocabulary, *tweet* is a term coined by the users, rather than the company — evidence of the playful loyalty that avid users have with the Twitter brand. In fact, it wasn't until late winter 2010 that Twitter officially adjusted updates to tweets, based on how the world talked about tweeting.

Twitter limits the length of tweets to 140 characters (letters, numbers, symbols, and spaces), a length that may seem short at first. And it is. How in the heck are you supposed to say anything in this tiny bit of space? How can you distill your company pitch into 140 characters, review a book, or summarize a movie in so few words? With time, you get used to this length restriction. Perhaps one of the coolest things about Twitter is that the more you use it, the easier it is to write short, sharp, clear tweets. As you get more accustomed to tweeting, you find that squeezing thoughts into 140 characters often makes you refine the point in ways you wouldn't have thought of before.

Some Twitter users have reported becoming better salespeople offline, or better writers, because Twitter's mandated brevity forces you to focus your thoughts into concise, direct sound bites. Because Twitter's communication format encourages brief but engaging ideas, Twitter sparks conversations faster than almost any other Internet conversation format.

Saying Hello! Your First Tweets

The entire premise of Twitter is to answer the question "What's happening?" in 140 characters or less. So, go ahead! Tell Twitter what's happening. Type a message in the text box directly below What's Happening?, keeping under the 140-character limit. When you're done, click Update. Congratulations! You just made your first tweet.

If you're thinking, "Wait, that's it?" That's right: that's it. Tweeting is that simple. Although your first tweet was probably something mundane, such as, "Trying out this Twitter thing" or "Hello there, Twitter. I'm reading *Twitter For Dummies!*", there's something more interesting going on.

While you start to add more and more tweets, people can begin to see what's going on in your life and what you're thinking about. Twitterers following you or searching for keywords in Twitter, in all likelihood, start talking to you about what you're doing. The conversation starts with those simple exchanges: Talk about your favorite band's new album, your mechanic and how she fixed your car's catalytic converter, or really anything at all. If you've already found your contacts on Twitter, they probably respond to you pretty quickly. If you don't have any followers yet, don't worry; they'll come.

We discuss suggested Twitter etiquette, culture, language, and all that stuff in Chapter 2. This chapter simply tells you how to get your Twitter profile up and running so that it reflects who you are and what you want to get out of Twitter.

Your tweets, right now, are publicly visible and searchable, even if you delete them immediately after hitting Update. This situation isn't life or death, but be careful. If your updates are unprotected, what you tweet ends up in Twitter Search and on Bing, and on Google, sometimes even if you delete it almost immediately.

Chapter 2

Getting Your Tweet Wet

. . . .

In This Chapter

▶ Following people

▶ Scouring Twitter for interesting people to follow

▶ Replying to messages, privately and publicly

▶ Attracting new followers

. . . .

*O*ne of the neatest byproducts of the Twitter experience is that your conversations, your followers, and your ability to interact with your network extends far past the Twitter.com interface into other platforms and even into the real world because of Twitter's ability to facilitate communications to plan both formal and spontaneous events. But equally important to accessing your Twitter account from virtually anywhere is understanding how to interact within the community.

In this chapter, we go over the nuts and bolts involved in discovering, managing, and interacting with your network: the people you follow on Twitter and the people who follow you. Additionally, we give you some hints about how to play well with others within the twitterverse so that you can start having conversations right away!

Finding People to Follow

A key part of getting the most out of Twitter is know-ing where and how to find people whose Twitter streams are of interest to you. Most people start by following friends, associates, and people they know. However, millions of people use Twitter, so you might consider scouring Twitter.com for other people who can add value to your stream.

You can easily find and follow people on Twitter: You naturally browse to people's profiles when you think that something they say is interesting or relevant to you. But, when you start accumulating updates from the people you follow, you'll quickly realize that you need to figure out who's worth following. That process can become complicated because of the large size and diversity of the Twitter ecosystem.

Avid users have countless theories and strategies about the best ways and reasons to follow others. But, remember that Twitter is for your use, so you can make up your own rules as you go along, creating your own criteria for building up a Twitter stream, which we talk about more in Chapter 3.

Twitter is a very personalized experience. No two people use Twitter in exactly the same way, and no two people follow a given account on Twitter for exactly the same reasons. Quite liter-ally, no two people experience the same Twitter because everyone is consuming different streams, and publishing to, and interacting with, different sets of readers.

Twitter is not a single village, as the term *Twitterville* implies. When Laura wrote "Twitter is my Village," (http://pistachioconsulting.com/it-takes-a-village-to-understand-twitter), she meant that each twitterer's personal community on Twitter functions like a village. Even now that Twitter has entered the mainstream, you're still able to shape your experience by selecting who you listen to and interact with.

As you become better at your entire Twitter experience, you naturally develop and change your own guidelines for building your network. Luckily, Twitter is built to allow for these changes, so you don't have to miss a beat.

Whether you're looking for business associates, news sources, friendly conversation, or anything else, Twitter can help you surround yourself with people and companies that can enrich your stream.

Look who's talking

When you want to start looking for people to follow, see whether anyone's already talked back to you. If you've already posted some tweets, people may have replied to you. (If you haven't yet tweeted, what are you waiting for? Dive in and start tweeting!)

When someone wants to address you directly on Twitter, that user does so by replying to you. They simply put the @ symbol before your Twitter handle at the beginning of a tweet — that's all it takes to reply. As a subtle point, if someone includes your name preceded by an @ symbol anywhere in their tweet, it's more generally considered an @-mention. Either way, you can view any tweets that mention you on the Mentions tab in the sidebar (it's the tab with @ followed by your username on it), assuming that those tweets are public or the person mentioning you has authenticated you to view their tweets (if their account is private).

reply

mention

If you're completely new to Twitter and you've posted only a handful of tweets, you probably won't have any mentions yet. That's okay! You have plenty of other options for finding people to follow (see the next sections).

Searching for people

You can best search for people on Twitter by using one of two methods: searching from the Twitter navigation bar (also called the "Search box") or clicking #Discover (see Figure 2-1).

Figure 2-1: Search for Twitter users on the People Search page.

Another, lesser-known way to find people on Twitter is by simply using the Google search engine at www.google.com. Because Google indexes every public tweet, you can use it to find twitterers by interest or by name. To use Google to find twitterers that you might want to follow, either search their firstname, lastname, and the word Twitter, or do a slightly more specific search this way:

1. **Type your keywords or the username you're looking for in the text box.**

2. **Add** site:Twitter.com **at the end of your search query.**

3. **Click the Search button.**

    See what pops up! Figure 2-2 shows the results of a search for Conan O'Brien.

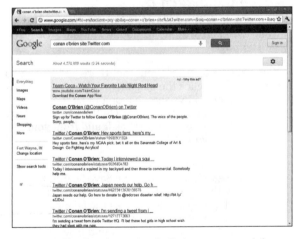

Figure 2-2: The Google results of a Twitter user search for Conan O'Brien.

You probably want to conduct people searches and keyword searches periodically to make sure that you continue to cultivate your Twitter experience's richness and value with new voices. Although Twitter is great for reconnecting with old friends and keeping up a conversation with existing business associates, it's also a fantastic way to reach out and find new people and companies to listen to.

A great way to get started following people on Twitter is to import your contacts from your web-based e-mail account (like Yahoo! Mail or Gmail).

Using the Search Box

Twitter makes it really easy to search for people using the main Search box, found at the top of every Twitter page.

You can type anything you want there and when you press enter or click the magnifying glass, your Twitter feed turns into a live search result of all the tweets that match your search query. On the left side of the page are the people Twitter has found from your search (see Figure 2-3).

If this is a search you think you'll do often, you can save that search by clicking the Save Search button marked by the gear symbol on the upper-right corner of the feed. (You can also access the advanced search here.) That saved search term sits under the Search field at the top of the page. Click in the Search field to see it.

Figure 2-3: Fast Twitter search for the Grammy award winning Adele.

Inviting people personally, through Twitter

Another option for inviting people to Twitter is to do it personally, directly to their individual e-mail addresses.

You can find this button (Invite Friends) on the Find Friends page (as shown in Figure 2-4), and it gives you a way to hand-pick people from your e-mail address book. You can also text Twitter at 40404 at any time with the words **invite *yourfriend@yourfriend*.com**, substituting your friend's e-mail address, of course.

Twitter doesn't offer you a chance to customize what the e-mail says. The person or company you invite gets a generic e-mail that mentions your Twitter handle and some basic information about how to sign up for an account. If you have people you want to invite to Twitter whom you think may not respond well to a generic e-mail, you can use the upcoming method to invite them, instead.

Figure 2-4: The Twitter Find Friends page.

The main drawback to any of the invitation options in Twitter's web interface is that none of them offer a custom message option. If you know people whom you want to invite, and you think they'd respond better to a private or more personalized note, just shoot them a normal e-mail that includes a link to the Twitter main page (www.twitter.com) and a note about

why they might benefit from signing up and joining in. It's often more effective to e-mail them a
link to an article that is going to help them
understand the uses of Twitter they may find
valuable. Twitter is definitely a minute-to-learn,
lifetime-to-master type of system.

Checking out Twitter Lists

One of Twitter's more personal features is the ability
for users to create lists of accounts. Unsurprisingly,
they're called Lists, and they can provide some struc-
ture to the people that you follow by allowing you to
categorize them.

NB — visible to others who look at your profile

For example, you may have a few different types of
people you follow: some are celebrities, some are
friends you went to school with, others are people
you work with. By using the Lists feature, you can
assign those people to lists. You can view these lists
as discrete Twitter streams so that when you view
them, the only tweets that show up are from the
people in that list.

You can use this feature to your advantage when finding other Twitter users to follow. For example, if a
classmate of yours has found you on Twitter, you may
visit her profile and notice that she's created a list of
people that went to your alma mater. By clicking that
list, you can see the usernames of everyone she has
found on Twitter who went to your school. Or, your
news-junkie friend may have a list of the best breaking-
news Twitter accounts. You can go into that list,
curated by your friend, and select the breaking news
outlet that works best for you.

check out other peoples lists

In short, you can use other people to help find
accounts that can add value to your experience.

If you find a list that you really enjoy, you can add that list to your own List collection.

Following back

By default, Twitter sends you an e-mail every time someone follows you. This is a useful starting point for finding people to follow because there's likely a reason why they followed you in the first place. It may be because they know you, or it may be because they think you're a good person to follow. Either way, it's nice to know when someone's following you.

Twitter.com, like any popular online communication tool, has spammers. Although Twitter has aggressively fought spam accounts, they still crop up from time to time. They're pretty easy to spot, usually offering you the usual fare of online deals or bedroom-related drugs. You can safely ignore them, but if you'd like to help Twitter identify these accounts, you can click the Block and Report for Spam button on their profiles.

If you find receiving Twitter notices a bother, you can turn them off:

1. **Click the person icon on your main page and choose Settings.**

   The Settings page opens.

2. **Click the Notifications link (see Figure 2-5).**

   You see a list of e-mail notification options.

3. **Select any of the e-mails you'd rather not receive.**

Figure 2-5: On the Notifications screen, you can choose which, if any, e-mails are sent to your mailbox.

Following People

Mechanically, following people on Twitter is dead simple. After you navigate to a person's Profile page, click the Follow button just below her avatar. And, you're done! Give it a shot:

1. **Browse to** http://twitter.com/dummies.

2. **Click the Follow button.**

   The button changes to the word Following. Cool!

Alternatively, you can post this message from SMS or any Twitter interface by typing **Follow username** or **F username**.

Following people on Twitter is straightforward. On the most superficial level, you just have to pay attention. Twitter is full of thousands of great conversations going on all around you. If you open yourself up to them, you may find that hundreds of excellent people are thrilled to meet you.

Replying to Tweets

So, what happens when you receive an @reply, and you want to respond — or if you just want to respond to any tweet, for that matter? Hover your mouse cursor over the right side of the tweet in question when you see it in your stream on Twitter's home screen, and a small handful of icons appears (as shown in Figure 2-6).

Figure 2-6: Don't miss the Reply arrow!

Click the Star icon to bookmark that tweet as a favorite, and click the Arrow icon to set up the Twitter entry field so that you can reply to that individual tweet. When you send your response, it reads In Reply To, below the tweet and includes a live link to the standalone page (also known as a *permalink*) for the tweet you responded to. Figure 2-7 shows a typical Twitter @reply.

Figure 2-7: You can respond to tweets with @replies.

You may find these permalinks helpful because Twitter isn't great at threading tweets together by conversation. If you're familiar with a set of @replies and the links associated with them, you can much more easily navigate the conversation later. When you know how to access the individual page for each tweet, you can also link to that tweet directly if you choose to respond to it in a longer format outside of Twitter, such as a blog post.

You can reply to any tweet that you can see, and the procedure is the same, whether you're following the person or not. But, assuming that your Twitter account is public, your @replies are public, too. If you want to use Twitter for private messages, the protocol is a little different, as we talk about in the next chapter.

Retweeting

In the early days of Twitter, it was commonplace for people not to just reply to tweets they liked, but to also forward that tweet on to their own followers. This practice grew to be known as retweeting (RT or R/T for short) and was so popular that Twitter built that functionality directly into its interface.

To retweet a link, follow these steps:

1. **Hover over the tweet that you'd like to forward to your followers.**

2. **Click the Retweet button.**

To your followers, that tweet looks as if it came from the person who wrote the tweet in the first place, complete with their avatar picture and username. To credit you for the retweet, Twitter places your name directly below the tweet.

If the user marked his updates as private, you won't see the retweet button. However, you can, of course, retweet them as you would before Twitter implemented the Retweet feature.

Retweeting the old-fashioned way

Although the Retweet feature is pretty neat, some users prefer the old way of doing things. (In fact, some Twitter API applications, which we cover in later chapters, don't include the retweet functionality, so it's good to know what the manual RT looks like in these cases.)

To retweet someone's tweet, simply retype or copy and paste that tweet into your Tweet prompt at the top of the page and format it like so:

RT @dummies This Tweet was written so you can practice retweeting.

Some people prefer to retweet this way:

This Tweet was written so you can practice retweeting. (via @dummies)

 Twitter etiquette says to make every effort to credit the original speaker of the tweet. When reviewing Twitter, many readers will read the beginning of the tweet and ignore the remainder or anything in parentheses following the tweet. Therefore, some think recognizing the speaker upfront is more polite.

Commentary on the retweet

Retweeting the old-fashioned way has some advantages. One compelling reason is that users can comment on the original message. Using Twitter's built-in retweet function, that's not possible because the original message is preserved and forwarded as-is. Therefore, to add commentary, you must either write it in another Tweet and link to the original, or use the old RT method if there's room for comment.

see next page for examp

For example, one might say:

@neilarmstrong: That's one small step for man, one giant leap for mankind.

Only to be retweeted with addendum:

> *@buzzaldrin: That was supposed to be "a man".*
> *Sheesh! RT @neilarmstrong That's one small step*
> *for man, one giant leap for mankind.*

(Note: We are as certain that these Twitter accounts
are those of the famous astronauts as we are that the
moon landing wasn't faked in a Hollywood basement.)

Twitter Directories

To be honest, we, the *Twitter For Dummies* team,
simply can't compete with timeliness or thorough-
ness of some online websites when it comes to finding
the buzzworthy people to follow for you. Thankfully,
Twitter.com and a number of sites have made finding
popular users even easier.

Twitter.com has a built-in list of suggested users (see
Figure 2-8). In the top navigation bar, click #Discover
and then the Browse Categories link, and Twitter will
break out a number of users you can follow based on
category.

From here, you can easily find the popular and prolific users who match the kind of Twitter stream you
want to cultivate.

Additionally, a number of third-party Twitter user
directories have grown popular over the years. One
favorite is WeFollow (www.wefollow.com), shown
in Figure 2-9, which not only lists popular Twitter
accounts to follow, but ranks them as well. It also
features the ability to sort and search for users based
on tags.

Figure 2-8: Twitter users who are of and are relating to Art & Design.

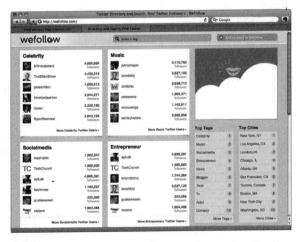

Figure 2-9: WeFollow: A comprehensive Twitter user list.

For example, if you want to search for authors, you can type **Authors** in the Search box on top and find all the users, ranked loosely by influence. If you want, you can add yourself to WeFollow. Just click the upper-right button and follow the instructions onscreen.

Understanding Twitter Protocol

Many Twitter neophytes want to know what the rules are or if Twitter has standard protocol and etiquette. Like many other social media sites, Twitter sprang from a close-knit group of early adopters who set the rhythm. Because Twitter was a favorite of Silicon Valley's new-media elite long before it broke into the mainstream, some insider jokes and conventions used can be confusing; however, they have since become part of the lexicon. Longtime users have certainly fallen into certain habits or sets of rules. But, remember, Twitter is what you make of it, and you are free to do your own thing.

Like any other social media company, Twitter has a Terms of Service (TOS) agreement that all members must adhere to or risk having their accounts suspended or deleted. You can access Twitter's terms at http://twitter.com/tos. You won't find anything particularly surprising in there.

Beyond the Terms of Service, there are Twitter Rules that provide guidelines against impersonation, threatening people, and other types of unwelcome behavior. To find these rules, navigate to the Twitter Help Center and search for The Twitter Rules.

Aside from the hard and fast terms and rules, Twitter etiquette is simple: Be genuine and nondeceptive and provide value. Other than that, just use Twitter how it suits you. Consider this an unofficial code of conduct (although, they're more like guidelines). But, do keep in mind that Twitter keeps tabs on "deceptive" activity: Twitter can and will ban accounts that impersonate celebrities or companies if those accounts don't make it clear that they're unofficial or parodies. This policy is a contentious point in the Twitter community: Many members were upset when the @cwalken account, belonging to an aspiring comedian pretending to be actor Christopher Walken, was deleted from the system.

Beyond the simple regulations, you can't really use Twitter in a right or wrong way because no two people use it for exactly the same reasons. But some members certainly have their opinions:

- ✔ Some users complain when others tweet too often, whereas others complain that their contacts don't tweet enough. (This complaint is a little silly. Don't like the contents? Turn the dial. Use a third-party tool. Unsubscribe.)

- ✔ Some users take issue with strings of @replies and wonder why those conversations weren't conducted in a private forum.

- ✔ You may encounter confusing, even conflicting, advice and back-seat tweeting from the handful of people on Twitter who aren't comfortable without rules. Don't take them too seriously: Twitter itself just isn't that rigid. Your Twitter community will help define your standard.

Be polite on Twitter, for the most part, but no more or less so than you're expected to be in the real world — just keep in mind that Twitter is a public forum. Twitter posts and feeds get exported outside of Twitter and onto Twitter-based websites, blogs, social media sites such as Facebook, and aggregators such as FriendFeed. If you know you plan to, say, sync your Twitter account with your Facebook account so that your tweets appear as your Facebook status message, keep in mind that you're branching out beyond the Twitter community and culture. (See the next chapter for a bit more on this.)

Although users love Twitter's largely rule-free nature, some generally accepted behaviors have evolved over time. You can ease your transition into the culture of Twitter by getting familiar with these behaviors and speech tendencies before you first start out. Establish dedication and credibility early on, in part, by knowing your way around the following Twitter customs.

Deciphering language and abbreviations

Over time, any group of people that interacts regularly falls into its own "vernacular" way of talking. Twitter is no exception to that rule; in fact, it may be even more subject to it because of the 140-character limit. Twitter's lexicon has evolved over time to include unique words, phrases, and abbreviations that most regular users understand and recognize. But new users often find these references confusing.

Right off the bat, you see a lot of puns involving the word "Twitter," with the prefixes tw- or twi- added to the front: tweet, tweeple, tweetup, and so on. At first, it looks like baby talk — and indeed, it can get a bit over-the-twop. (See our point?) Not all members are fans of corny terms such as tweeple. Others think the Twitter-specific language is fun, or an easy and obvious way to delineate something as Twitter-specific. Either way, whether you plan to use goofy Twitter-speak or not, it does help to know what this stuff means.

Many application and website names have adopted Twitter-speak words for products and services associated with Twitter or that tap into Twitter's application programming interface (API) to use Twitter data. For example, the word *twinfluence* was used casually to describe (no shock here) the kind of social influence that individual Twitter users had within the Twitter community. Eventually, the slang term was used to name twInfluence (www.twinfluence.com), an application that gets its data from Twitter and turns it into a report that estimates Twitter users' power and influence.

Plenty of eccentric people use Twitter, not to mention loads of subcultures and subcommunities. Just because you see an unfamiliar term doesn't mean it's part of the Twitter vernacular.

Engaging others on Twitter

On Twitter, the name of the game is engagement. Whether you use Twitter for business or fun, you don't just want to sit back and watch the stream flow by — you want to genuinely interact with people. You have to know how to listen as much as know how to converse (this goes twice for businesses) — but it always boils down to engagement.

Okay, you don't absolutely have to engage people on Twitter. But, we think your Twitter experience will become a lot more fruitful if you do.

First and foremost, do not be shy about finding people who share your interests, even if you don't know them (yet). Use http://search.twitter.com to look for some of the most obscure keywords related to your work, hobbies, or passions. Then click through to the profiles of the people who wrote the tweets you find. You'll be amazed how good an idea you get of someone just by glancing at their last 20 tweets. Interested? Follow them. It's not like other social networks where you're really only expected to connect to folks you already know.

While you sift through the Twitter conversation, don't be shy about clicking the usernames that you see (as in @replies) and writing to strangers offering your own opinion. It may take some time through several conversations before the chatting users include you in their conversation, but if you're adding to the conversation, they will.

But even if you don't @reply, your tweets still appear in Search, and other Twitter users can spot them. If you have something interesting to say, people start to reply to your tweets. If you seek out and use relevant keywords and #hashtags, you will start to connect with others who share your interests. Your early days on Twitter will probably be pretty quiet when it comes to replies and conversation. All those twitterers are just getting to know you, after all. Don't worry; after a few of your tweets appear in the timeline and you add a few contacts to your network, people will begin to notice you.

Tweeting frequency

Twitter users tend to settle into a rhythm of tweeting frequency, often unconsciously, over time. Some Twitter users are considered noisy because they tweet so much, whereas others can come across as standoffish because they don't tweet frequently. So, how much is too much or too little? How often should you tweet?

A good rule when you're starting out is to post at least four or five tweets per day. You most likely find yourself tweeting much more often than that, but if you aren't yet fully comfortable with it, four or five should get you going at a good, unobtrusive, and value-adding pace.

If you're using Twitter for your business, or you plan to link to your products or posts on your personal blog, find a balance between the number of tweets that promote yourself and the number of tweets that provide value. You might think of this balance as an actual ratio. For example, for every link of your own that you place on Twitter, send out at least five tweets that inform, engage, and converse. If conversation and engagement are your aim, you definitely want to keep a human voice in your Twitter stream at all times.

In short: talk with people, not at them.

It's worth thinking about who you want to reach. People new to Twitter and only following a few get bowled over by frequent tweeters simply because it's all they see on their stream. A roaring chat with friends you already know is a fine use of Twitter, too, and would involve *many* more tweets a day than, say, a business user or someone just figuring out what they want to do with the platform.

Creating Lists

As you start using Twitter more frequently, you may notice that you've followed quite a few accounts and are looking for a better way to manage the content flooding through your Twitter.com feed. One of

Twitter's more helpful features — Lists — helps you do just that.

One thing you might notice is that your less Internet-happy friends get lost in the wash of your Twitter. com feed. Between the news agencies, celebrities, and the generally prolific, it's your quieter, more personal friends who are probably the tweets that deserve your individual attention. Well, by creating lists, you can separate those out from the noise.

You can also create themed lists, say, a list of TV personalities, Nobel Laureates, or billionaires. But, some of our favorite uses for lists are to make sure the important people in our lives aren't lost in the noise.

Creating a list is easy. Log in, click the person icon (beside the Search box) and select Lists, and in the side column within your main page, you see a Lists section below the Tweets, Following, Followers, and Favorites links. Click Create List in the main window, give it a name ("Book club"), a description ("These are my friends who I share book tweets with"), and mark it as private or public. If you don't want anyone else to access the list, set your list to private.

Click Save List, and you're taken to a page where you can search for users to add to your list. Although this way works for you if you're creating a list around a searchable criteria (like if you were building a list of microsharing not-for-profits or professional tennis players), it's a bit clunky if you're trying to manage your friends.

Instead, click the Following link in your sidebar to get to the page detailing the people you follow. To add a user to your newly created list, click the person icon on the right of the person you want to add, and select Add or Remove From Lists. Click the check box next to the list name, and — presto! — your friend is now on your list.

Private lists are for your eyes only; not even the people on the list know they're on it. Public lists, on the other hand, are accessible to everyone on Twitter.

You probably noticed that you can also create lists right from that drop-down list. That will work exactly the same way, and it's a handy way to make lists on the fly. For example, you might want to spend some time going through your existing Following page and categorize some of the people you're following. In fact, they'll probably appreciate it, and here's why:

Whenever you list someone on a public list, his Listed count goes up by one, along with a notification of what that list is called. Say you want to keep tabs on people you think are interesting; you could create an "Interesting People" list and add @gruen to it. (That is, of course, if you think he's interesting.) Now, when you browse to @gruen's profile page (twitter.com/gruen) and see the people who have listed him, you notice not only that Interesting People has him listed, but you can also see how other Twitter users have chosen to list him. From here, you can get a better sense of who this person is and why people have chosen to follow and list him.

You need not follow users to add them to lists! Just visit *their* profile page and use their person icon to access the List menu. Add them accordingly.

When choosing whether or not to follow someone, having been listed under relevant or interesting lists can help a user's credibility and identity on Twitter.

Keep your list names innocuous. If you create a list called "Funny while intoxicated," your boss may or may not approve of your listing her on that list. She might be inclined to block you and your list from following her, and you might burn a bridge in the process. Then again, your boss might find that hysterical (even when not intoxicated), so you need to use your best judgment.

Following lists

Whenever anyone creates a public list, that list can be found on the user's profile page on the side column under Lists. Notice that those lists are constructed strangely: They contain the user's name, followed by a forward slash, followed by the list name. This is because like users, lists have their own profile pages and, like users, can be followed.

For example, if you wanted to follow Laura, Leslie, and Michael's collective antics, you could follow the @dummies/authors list (`http://twitter.com/dummies/authors`). By clicking the Follow This List button, you can follow that list, and a link to that page will show up under your Lists section in your own landing page's sidebar.

You won't, however, automatically follow each one of us individually or collectively. Our tweets will reside only in that list unless you explicitly follow us. Additionally, if a member of a list has protected his tweets, you'll need to follow him and get authorization to follow his tweets in order to get his updates on the list page.

To unfollow a list, return to that list page and find the Unfollow link, which you can find at the upper-right corner of the list's main feed.

Using geolocation

If you'd like, you can tweet on-location and demon-
strate that you are where you say you are! One of
Twitter's newer features is the ability to add location
data to your tweet. Although it's not terribly exciting
while you're sitting at your desk and using the web
version of Twitter, Twitter mobile clients (and the
`mobile.twitter.com` site) can, at your option, add
your location information to your tweet.

If you have a smartphone, visit `mobile.twitter.`
`com` and sign in. Directly under the Tweet prompt,
notice an option to turn on location information.

Alternatively, a number of third-party applications
use the Twitter API and can report on information.
For example, the mobile check-in application
Foursquare (`foursquare.com`) lets you tell both
Foursquare friends and Twitter followers where you
are at any time you want to let them know. When
Foursquare forwards that information to post onto
Twitter, the location information will be embedded
into the tweet data, like a timestamp. (We cover third-
party applications in Chapter 6.)

On the bottom of the tweet in Figure 2-10, Twitter tells
you some information about that tweet: when it happened, how it happened, and where it happened. If
you visit that tweet's URL

```
http://twitter.com/dummies/
status/11329511402
```

you'll be able to click the location part of the tweet
and see the map, as shown.

Figure 2-10: A location-based Tweet.

Twitter itself asks for and displays your city or neighborhood, like Detroit, Michigan. If you want to be specific, as in Figure 2-10, you have to use a third-party app.

Erasing your tracks

If you find yourself needing to get rid of your location information for whatever reason, Twitter can strip the location information out of all your tweets.

To wipe all location-data from your tweets

1. **Click the person icon from the navigation bar along the top and choose Settings.**

2. **On the Account page, scroll down until you see Tweet Location.**

3. **Click the Delete All Location Information button.**

It may take up to 30 minutes for Twitter to extricate you from your location history. Good luck.

Deciphering Twitter SMS Commands

The more you use Twitter with your mobile phone, the more you're going to want to find quicker ways to do things. Conveniently, Twitter has included a number of shorthand codes that you can use to perform almost any action directly from the Tweet box.

 Be careful when using shorthand code! Making a typo when you want to send a direct (private) message can send an update to everyone who follows you. It's smart to be particularly careful about sending sensitive information via direct messages, just in case. At some point, you might accidentally share something with everyone that you intended only a particular user to see. Best bet? Use the actual message link on a person's page to send them a direct message.

Sending a direct message

You can send a direct message (DM) right from the Update box by using the following form:

D *username message*

In this message, *username* is the username of the person whom you want to direct message, and *message* is any message that you want to send. So, if you want to tell us how great this book is, you type in the What Are You Doing? box:

> **D dummies I am really enjoying Twitter For Dummies! Thanks for the help!**

Many users opt to have direct messages sent straight to their cellphones via SMS and/or e-mail, so you can frequently use direct messages to reach someone instantly even if you don't have a cell number or if you know that he's an active Twitter user who may not be online at the moment. Some make heavy use of this while traveling and at events and find it much easier to coordinate on the fly.

Sending a follow message

No matter what application or interface you use to tweet, you can quickly add a twitterer to your feed just by sending an update to Twitter. Say that you decide to follow the updates of Evan Williams (@ev), Twitter's cofounder and CEO. Just send this message to Twitter:

> **F ev**

Alternatively, you can type the word **follow** to do the exact same thing:

> **follow ev**

When you add someone using the `follow` or `f` command, you both follow them and opt in to receive their individual device updates (only when your account is set to receive device updates). When you follow them using the website Follow button or most

Twitter clients, you connect only via the website, not also via SMS device updates.

Sending an @reply

We cover how to reply to users in the "Replying to Tweets," section, but the @ symbol is really a short-hand for referencing another Twitter user. The difference between this command and all other commands is that there is *no* space between it and the username of the person you want to reach. Want to say something to Leslie? Write

@leslie hiya!

Twitter makes sure that the message ends up in Leslie's Mentions tab.

Using On/Off commands

The commands On and Off control whether or not your entire account will receive device updates (SMS texts on your phone). You can use the On command to turn device updates on for your account. To turn them off, you can use the Off command by sending Twitter the update **off.**

Making a tweet a favorite

If something someone just tweeted made you laugh (say, our @dummies account), you can favorite that tweet by sending an update to Twitter:

fav dummies

If you're receiving updates on your cellphone, sending **fav** by itself adds the last update you received to your Favorites tab on your home screen.

Seeing stats

If you ever want to know how many followers you
have and how many users you're following, send the
update **stats.** If you're online, Twitter displays a message at the top of the screen letting you know. If you
sent **stats** from your cellphone, Twitter sends you a
text message with your stats in it. Obviously this
makes a lot more sense than viewing stats on the web
page, where they are, of course, already displayed.
Stats was a little more meaningful with Track because
it also reminded you what words you were tracking.

Using the Get command

The Get command allows you to quickly view the last
update from a user. Want to see Michael's latest
tweet? Send to Twitter

   get gruen

And Twitter will report back with Michael's last tweet.
However, we find this example particularly ironic as
nobody really "gets" him.

Seeing profiles with Whois

If you want to get someone's profile information
quickly (say, Laura's), use the Whois command:

   whois pistachio

Twitter sends you a message that contains the user's
proper name (Laura Fitton), how long she's been on
Twitter (since April 2007), and her current bio from her
Profile page (http://twitter.com/pistachio).

Using Leave

Leave seems like it would be the opposite of follow, but it's not — at least, not quite. **Leave username** simply turns off the individual's device updates, those text messages that some twitterers receive on their phones; it does not unfollow that person on Twitter.

Using On/Off username

Not to be confused with On/Off (see the earlier section), **On/Off username** turns device updates on and off for individual users. Like follow, On will also connect you to people on Twitter.com so that you're following their updates. And like the leave command, the Off username command stops device updates, but it doesn't unfollow the username account.

In other words, **On/Off username** has no unique functionality that is different from Follow/Leave.

Using Quit and Stop

The Quit and Stop commands discontinue all service between Twitter and your cellphone. They opt your cellphone number out of Twitter altogether. If used, you'll literally have to log in to your Twitter account and redo the steps to add your cellphone to your account.

These commands are probably not the best options to quiet your phone. They're handy though if you accidentally lock your phone into a separate account by sending **join** to 40404 after you already have an account.

Codes may come, and codes may go

Because Twitter is a living application, it has commands that come and go. Of note, you may still see some older Twitter users lamenting the loss of the Track feature.

For a recent list of Twitter commands, browse to Twitter's Help forums by clicking the Help link at the top of every Twitter page. At time of print

```
https://support.twitter.com/articles/
14020-twitter-for-sms-basic-features
```

has the most accurate list of Twitter SMS commands.

Chapter 3

Flying Around the Interface

. . . .

In This Chapter

▶ Reading the feed on your Twitter home screen

▶ Making a Twitter conversation personal by using
  @replies and direct messages

▶ Marking your Twitter favorites

▶ Viewing who you're following and who's following you

▶ Reviewing your Twitter updates

. . . .

*F*or the power it wields, Twitter is one of the sim-
plest — and, we think, most elegant — websites
for mass communication. The interface makes interacting with other people — some you already know,
and others you'll meet — incredibly easy, and it
cleanly organizes a lot of information.

As you use Twitter more and more, you'll likely want
to know where to locate its features quickly and
manage your communication flow more intelligently.
In this chapter, we dive down into each Twitter page
view, showing how it relates to the conversations
going on around you as well as the conversations
you're having directly.

Starting Out on the Home Screen

When you first log into Twitter, the home screen is your first stop. After you set up your account, you go to this screen to touch base with your followers and the people you're following. On the home screen, you can also see who's talking to you directly through @replies (tweets in response to individual users) and direct messages (DMs; private, one-to-one tweets). For more on using @replies and DMs, see the upcoming sections, "Tweeting to One Specific Person: @Replies" and "Sending Private Notes via Direct Messaging."

Additionally, use controls along the top of the home screen to change your settings, update your profile background, upload your avatar, toggle your SMS notifications, and more. (Chapter 1 covers most of these setup features.)

The home screen, shown in Figure 3-1, has a standard layout. The header has a Twitter logo in the center and a list of links to the left and icons on the right, which appears on all Twitter pages. Those links' names describe where they take you:

- ✔ **Home:** Your home screen. Clicking here always takes you home.

- ✔ **@Connect:** Find out whether anyone has mentioned your username (@mention), has followed you, retweeted your tweet, or marked a tweet of yours as a favorite.

- ✔ **#Discover:** The Discover tab condenses a lot of activity. You'll see what people you follow are up to, suggestions on who to follow, stories, and trending content. You can also find more friends to follow from the Discover tab. It's about making your Twitter experience more productive.

- ✔ **Search:** Use this text-entry field for fast searching.

- ✔ **The "person icon":** Click this icon to access a quick menu. Click it to view your profile page, direct messages, and lists; get help; look at keyboard shortcuts; visit the Settings page (where you can configure your Twitter account); and sign out.

- ✔ **Compose new Tweet button:** Click to open a new What's happening? tweet window that works just like the tweet area below your stats.

Figure 3-1: The Twitter home screen, where you'll spend a lot of time.

Twitter is a living web application. Its interface changes from time to time, so if you can't find something immediately, it's likely taken on a different name or moved to a different location on the interface. For up-to-date information about what's going on with Twitter, visit the company's blog (http://blog.twitter.com).

The sidebar

The area on the left side of most Twitter.com screens (a column with blocks of information — yours on top) is the sidebar. It's both a reference for what you're looking at in the main content area and a controller for the website, and it's configured a little differently in each view. Here's a breakdown of what's on the sidebar. Except where noted, this description applies to the sidebar on your home screen:

✔ **Your information, stats, and Tweet box:** At the top of this area is your avatar picture and username. When you're logged in to Twitter and on your home screen, you'll see only your avatar and username. Your Name, Location, Web, or Bio appear only on your Profile page. Click your avatar, the Profile link, or any @username link for your name to see your Profile page.

Next comes your stats. You can see how many tweets you've sent, plus how many people are following you as well as how many people you're following, in nice bold numbers.

Finally, this area of the sidebar contains the Tweet box. This is where you tweet although you can also click the Compose New Tweet icon on the right side of the top menu bar to get tweeting.

✔ **Who to follow:** Next, you may see a Who to Follow section, with suggestions on, well, who to follow.

> ✔ **Worldwide trends:** The Worldwide Trends box
> shows you the most commonly tweeted words
> and hashtags at any given time. The view is a
> surprisingly powerful peek at what is going on in
> the world (at least, the world according to twit-
> terers) at any given moment. Click Change to
> focus on a specific country.

The Tweet box

Beneath your stats, you find a box in which you can
post your latest update (or tweet). If you continually
use Twitter's web interface to post updates, you'll
become very well acquainted with that box.

When you click in the box, it expands in size and adds
a few links beneath it you use to attach a photo and
add your location, and also a button to click to send
the tweet. Beside the Tweet button is a character
counter. While you type your message, that number
decreases, letting you know how many more characters you can type before you hit the limit. When you
get to 19 characters remaining, the number turns bur-
gundy; and when you get to 10 characters remaining,
the number turns red. If you go over 140 characters,
the number starts decrementing into the negatives. If
you can't click the Tweet button, you've gone over
the limit, so be succinct!

As soon as you type a new tweet and click the Tweet
button, your tweet appears at the top of the main
timeline on the right side of the page.

If your last tweet was on the long side, you might
notice that it was shortened and also that an ellipsis
(. . .) appears at the end of your tweet. If that's the
case, you can click that ellipsis to see your full tweet.
If you replied to anyone or included a link in your

tweet, you can now click that link. Additionally, the timestamp saying how long ago you posted that update contains that update's permalink. Click that link, and a page dedicated to that tweet — and that tweet alone — opens. Cool, huh?

 This seemingly subtle fact is a big part of what makes conversations on Twitter different. Unlike instant messaging (IM) or a chat room, every single tweet can be uniquely bookmarked, linked to, replied to, and archived. Right now, you can go online and view famous tweets you may have heard about, such as @JamesBuck's "Arrested" at

```
http://twitter.com/jamesbuck/
statuses/786571964
```

or @JanisKrum's "There's a plane in the Hudson . . ." at

```
http://twitter.com/jkrums/
status/1121915133
```

The Twitter stream

All the action on Twitter appears on the right side of your screen. This stream of Twitter updates is the main timeline. It contains your tweets and the tweets of those you follow in a chronological order, with the most recent tweets at the top.

The main timeline goes by several names, depending on who you're talking to and when they started using Twitter, including *stream, timeline,* or sometimes *feed* (not to be confused with RSS feeds, which you can read about in this chapter and Chapter 4). Some people who follow thousands of Twitter users call it a *river* — the tweet stream flows faster the more people

you add to your list of friends and the more people
you follow.

 The stream "flows" only when you refresh your
web browser; it doesn't automatically display
new tweets. Words like *stream* and *flow* most
likely derive from the more dynamic moving displays on many third-party Twitter clients.

This is where the conversations happen; it's your
home base for connecting with people and businesses
on Twitter. By reading your stream, you can find new
people to listen to (friends of your friends and connections) and a place to jump in and participate.

Each tweet appears in its own section of the timeline.
If you hover your cursor over the area, several icons
pop up on the right side of the tweet. These icons act
like function buttons:

✔ **Reply (arrow):** Reply is one of the most confusing names in Twitterdom. Don't confuse replying to a Tweet with replying to an e-mail. In the
latter case, you're assured that the person you
are replying to will receive the message. It goes
directly to them.

In this case, Reply is simply a public tweet that
begins with their username. If they don't follow
you, there's no reason to believe that they will
ever see it. In that case, they have to be savvy
enough to be looking for tweets that mention
them.

 Don't confuse replies with *mentions,* which
are tweets with a person's username anywhere in the body of the tweet.

✔ **Retweet (double arrow):** You can forward the
tweet you're reading to your Twitter followers
by clicking the Retweet button. Your Twitter

followers see that tweet as coming from the user who first said it, along with a note along the bottom of the tweet mentioning that the retweet came from you. (Note that if the tweet came from a user who protects his or her updates, this feature will be unavailable.)

✔ **Favorite (star):** Clicking the star button adds that tweet to your Favorites list (which you can get to by clicking Favorites on your Lists page). When you mark something as a favorite, you make it easier for yourself to find that tweet in the future.

✔ **Open (dot):** Clicking this icon expands the tweet and reveals the exact time it was sent, and how, and enables you to open it as its own page.

✔ **Delete (trash can):** This icon appears only with your tweets. Not surprisingly, clicking it lets you delete the tweet from the feed. (*Note:* If you're not seeing a trash can icon next to your own tweet, odds are that Twitter is working on something. Occasionally, the trash can icon disappears, and you have to wait to delete a tweet — all the more reason to make sure that you don't tweet anything you don't mean to tweet!)

Tweeting to One Specific Person: @Replies

The little arrow icon on the home screen that appears when you hover your mouse over a Tweet is the force behind one of Twitter's most powerful conversational features: @replies. Taking its format from a syntax used in text chat rooms, @replies is a tweet that although public and visible to all Twitter users, is

directed specifically to one Twitter user. Twitter has
ramped it up by automatically detecting when an
@ symbol is placed directly in front of a word (with no
space between) and adds a link to the Twitter user
who has that word as his or her handle. More than
just a way to direct a tweet to one person, @replies
can also help you find new people to add to your
network when you see one of your contacts convers-
ing with someone you don't know and decide to
check that person out.

For every publicly viewable tweet that includes a
user's handle, that user can view those tweets in the
@replies link. So, anytime your @username appears
in a tweet, it gets collected here. Some heavy users
don't like this setup because it can get cluttered fast
if you're lucky enough to get mentioned a lot. Even
though the page is now considered the Mentions
page, most Twitterers still call them @replies or
@mentions, so we use that here.

If you hover your cursor over the tweet that you want
to respond to, the arrow icon appears, which you can
then click to reply to that tweet. Clicking the arrow
icon makes the user's Twitter handle appear in the
Tweet box window (entitled In Reply To), followed by
the username of the person you're replying to — and
the Tweet button becomes, effectively, a Reply
button. Twitter then associates your reply with the
original tweet in the Twitter system. The person can
see what tweet prompted your reply by clicking the In
Reply To link at the bottom of your tweet to him. This
link is helpful, especially when you're responding to
people who are frequent Twitter users and may have
already put out more tweets since the one you're
replying to — it lets them see specifically what you're
responding to.

If you want to quickly see who is tweeting you, go to your Twitter Mentions page (like the one shown in Figure 3-2), which you can open by clicking the @Connect button and then the Mentions link.

Figure 3-2: The @mentions screen, where your ego can get a boost — or not.

@replies are public tweets. So, unlike text that you send in an IM program, which you may be used to, other people can always read your @replies, and they'll be stored by search engines. If you have something private that you need to tell someone, use another feature of Twitter, the direct message (DM, which we talk about in the following section).

Sending Private Notes via Direct Messaging

Direct messages (DMs) let you send your contacts private notes through Twitter. Just like regular tweets and @replies, DMs are limited to 140 characters. Unlike regular tweets and @replies, though, the only person who can see a DM is the recipient.

You can send a DM only to a Twitter user who's following you (although you don't have to be following that user), which is designed to prevent spamming and other unwanted messages by ensuring that people get direct messages only from people they actually want to follow.

The easiest way to see whether someone is following you and to send them a direct message while you're there is simply to go to that person's Profile page. You can get to the Profile page by either clicking that person's @username anywhere that you see it or by typing the username into the URL bar on your web browser after Twitter.com (http://twitter.com/ *username*). Then follow these steps:

1. **Click their person icon and select the Send a Direct Message link, as shown in Figure 3-3.**

   If the only action visible is to block the person, he does not follow you, and you can't DM him.

   The screen changes to a single text box, over the user's Twitter background, titled Direct Messages > New.

2. **Write and send your message.**

   Compose your direct message in this box and then click Send. As with routine tweets, you only have 140 characters to get your message across, as shown in Figure 3-4.

Figure 3-3: If you don't see this link, you can't DM the user in question.

Figure 3-4: Typing a new DM.

You can also send a DM from the main Direct Messages interface:

1. **Click your person icon at the top of the screen and select Direct Messages.**

   The Direct Messages page opens, displaying the DMs you've sent and a button to create new messages with.

2. **Click New Message to create a new DM.**

3. **Type in the @username of the person you want to message, and the message in the next window.**

You're limited to 140 characters, as usual.

4. **Click Send Message to send the DM.**

You can send DMs from any regular Twitter input source — text messages, third-party apps, or the main Twitter interface — by entering **d [username]** and then typing your tweet. For example, if you want to send a direct message to our Dummies account (@dummies) to ask when the next edition of *Twitter For Dummies* is coming out, you format the DM as

d dummies When's the next edition coming out?

Sending DMs is easy, but proceed with caution! Many Twitter users have embarrassing tales of DMs that they accidentally sent as public tweets because they formatted the tweet incorrectly or sent it from the Twitter home screen instead of from the user's Profile page (best bet) or the Direct Messages page. Double-check, just to be sure.

Playing (Twitter) Favorites

One of the icons that appear when you hover your mouse over a particular tweet is the Favorites star. It's basically Twitter's equivalent of a bookmarking tool, and twitterers often overlook it. When you mark a tweet as a favorite, it appears on your Favorites page (see Figure 3-5). You may want to mark a tweet as a favorite to

✔ Save it for later.

✔ Acknowledge that it helped you or that you found it amusing.

✔ Mark it so that you can reply to it later.

✔ Remember it so that you can reference it in a blog post or article.

✔ Save it to quote later.

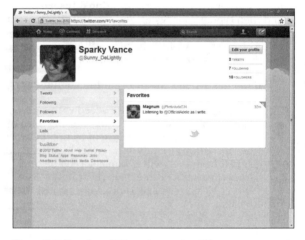

Figure 3-5: Your favorite tweets are stored forever.

Ari Herzog (@ariherzog) pointed out that favorites are an untapped opportunity to collect testimonials and other tweets that might have value for your company. Innovation software company Brightidea (@brightidea) uses it to curate a great collection of tweets about innovation, drawing upon Twitter search results for keywords related to innovation.

Our point is to not limit yourself to using Favorites only as literal favorites. Use Favorites whichever way works best for you!

 If you start using the Favorites icon on a regular basis, you'll soon have a large collection of tweets that you can gather data from for various projects or reference when you need to remember a particular joke or comment. You can also use it for bookmarking links so that you can visit it later — many of your best links and referrals will come from your fellow Twitter users.

 One way to find more people on Twitter is to visit the Profile pages of your friends on Twitter and look at *their* Favorites, to see which tweets they liked the most. If your best friend marked a particular tweet as a favorite, and you're not yet following the person who posted that tweet, you may want to start following that person.

Seeing Who You Follow

After you start using Twitter to its full potential, you may want to see a list of whom you follow. To see whom you follow

1. **Log in to Twitter.**

   On any page in Twitter, you find the sets of numbers labeled Tweets, Following, and Followers.

2. **From your home page, click Following.**

   A list of people you're following appears (as shown in Figure 3-6). Currently, Twitter sorts your Following list chronologically by when you started following them, with the most recent at the top.

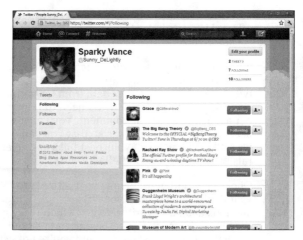

Figure 3-6: Check out the twitterers whom you're following.

3. **Scroll through the list manually, page by page.**

   This process works fine until you start to follow
   many more people. Without a way to sort or
   search — which Twitter still doesn't have (hint,
   hint, Twitter!) — finding out whether you follow
   someone specifically can become tedious after
   you start following more than 100 people.

 If you have a particular user in mind and
   you're not sure whether you're following
   him, go to that person's Twitter page. If
   you're following him, you'll see a large
   button labeled Following, near the top of the
   screen on the right side. If you're not following him, you'll see a Follow button, which
   you can click to follow him.

Who's Following Who?

You may also want to see who's following you on Twitter — maybe you want to find new people to follow, or you're just curious who's reading your tweets. You can pull up the list of your followers from your home page. Find the sets of numbers beneath your avatar labeled Tweets, Following, and Followers, and click Followers.

Similar to the Following link (which we talk about in the preceding section) the Followers link brings up a list of people who are following you. Twitter sorts the list with the people who've started following you the most recently at the top.

Just like the Following list, you can scroll through the entire list of Followers (see Figure 3-7). Check out tools like Friend or Follow (www.friendorfollow.com) that can show you both who you're following and who's following you, which is considerably easier than scrolling through your followers page by page.

If you don't want to have to constantly use a site such as Friend or Follow to keep up with your followers, you have several options:

- ✔ **Turn on e-mail notifications in the Settings area.** Click the Notifications tab, select the Email When I'm Followed by Someone New check box, and then click Save Changes. The e-mail notification authorizes Twitter to send you an e-mail alerting you about each new follower. Then, you can just click a link in the e-mail to that user's profile and see right away whether you want to follow them back.

- ✔ **Try to send a user who may be following you a direct message.** Find a tweet from that person or go to her profile page. Click her person icon and see whether you can send her a DM. If she is following you, you'll be able to send that DM. If that user isn't following you, you won't even see the menu. Then you have to decide whether you want to try to get that user's attention in another way.

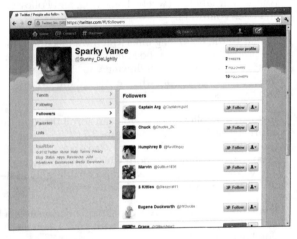

Figure 3-7: Your followers.

Reviewing Your Tweets

You can see what you've tweeted in the past in a variety of ways. The first place to check is your own profile: Click your avatar to open your Profile page. Your Profile page, in addition to displaying your short bio and profile information, displays a feed of all your public tweets in chronological order. Just like the

pages showing your followers and who you follow
(which you can read about in the preceding sections),
you can keep scrolling down to the bottom of the
page to see older posts.

Also, your profile is a publicly accessible URL. For
example, if your username is @dummies, navigate to
http://twitter.com/dummies to jump directly to
your Profile page.

If you're looking for a specific tweet, you can first look
for it by using Twitter's Advanced Search page. To
find it, conduct a search normally, and when you get
a results page, click the gear icon by the Search
button. Select Advanced Search to take you to this
well-hidden tool (see Figure 3-8) and then go crazy
with people, word, or hashtag searches with lots of
advanced options.

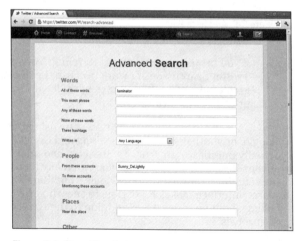

Figure 3-8: Searching for a tweet.

Figure 3-9 shows the results of the search.

Figure 3-9: And here it is.

 If you protect your updates, searching by using Twitter Search doesn't work because the tweets aren't indexed in the search engine. It's a small price to pay for privacy.

You can also search for specific tweets by using Bing, Google, or another search engine. Bing and Google actually purchase data from Twitter.com and offer advanced search terms so that you can really focus the search. Additionally, both Google's and Bing's search interface makes it possible to see who else is talking about your tweets, in addition to the tweets themselves.

 Google and Bing do such a good job of indexing Twitter that it remains (at this writing) the best way to find out whether someone is on Twitter.

At Bing or Google, run a search for Firstname
Lastname Twitter, and usually you can find out
right away whether a person is a tweeter. Bear
in mind that very famous people who appear to
be tweeting may be fan pages or other hoaxes,
though — unless @DarthVader actually does
exist — in which case, be very afraid!

Your public tweets are indexed by search
engines. You can delete your tweets on Twitter
by clicking the trash can icon, but if you don't
do it within a few seconds, Bing and other
search engines (as well as Twitter's own search
tool) have already indexed those tweets. So,
sometimes tweets are forever. On one hand, this
indexing is good for your visibility online.
Because Bing and other search engines index
your tweets, those search engines can bring
more people to your Twitter profile, which can
then possibly bring those people to your website. On the other hand, you need to be cautious: If you're tweeting as "you," we advise not
saying anything on Twitter that you wouldn't
want your mom, boss, or child to stumble across
later on the Internet while searching for something else. Also take great care with names,
because tweets about a person may actually
show up closer to the top of search results than
mentions of her name on other types of websites.

If you imagine that someone whose opinion you
value is looking at what you write, you can
avoid getting in any trouble. Twitter is so easy
to use that it's equally easy to slip up, and
because of its conversational nature, you can
sometimes forget that it isn't a private room,
and that it isn't an "inner monologue." A
Ketchum PR executive famously upset his client —
FedEx — when he tweeted a snide remark about
Memphis on landing there for his meeting with

them. Ooops! Remember the context you're tweeting in (he was on a client visit) and also remember that people may assume that you're talking about them when you're not. You also may not be thinking today about what may be findable weeks, months, and years from now.

You've Been Listed

Santa's not the only one who gets to check things twice these days. Twitter users also get to make lists of people. Being added to a list is kind of like being followed in that a user has identified you as a person to follow. But, instead of getting a new follower, Twitter identifies you as being a member of that list.

Someone may have listed you for a few reasons. You may have gone to school with that person. You may have met that person at an event, and they think you have entertaining tweets. In any case, you must have done something right for them to have listed you!

To see who's "listed" you (and what list you've been put on), click the person icon at the upper-right and choose Lists.

The list names are structured in a neat way: written as the user who made the list, followed by a slash, followed by the name of the list itself (see Figure 3-10).

What's particularly neat about this is that if you click on the list name, you'll see the stream of tweets written by the people in that list.

Lists add a little bit of complexity and subtlety to the Twitter experience, and they can be pretty powerful tools to help you manage your interests.

Figure 3-10: See where you've been listed.

The User Multi-Face: Interacting with Twitter Every Which Way

If you want to get the most out of Twitter, you need to figure out how you prefer to access the service. Some people use the Twitter website or the Twitter Mobile website, text messaging, or any number of third-party services built by using Twitter's application program interface (API). You can use widgets, gadgets, browser plug-ins — in short, a huge array of ways to interact with Twitter at your convenience and on your terms. This is a big reason for Twitter's popularity.

Like most users, you probably started by logging into Twitter.com and using the basic web interface, shown earlier in Figure 3-1, to manage your Twitter stream and communicate with your contacts. It's simple, no-frills, and convenient: Most of what you need is right there in the sidebar or in the top toolbar, and roughly half of all twitterers (probably more now with Twitter's extraordinary recent growth) use Twitter. com to access the service. But what happens if you need more functionality, mobility, versatility, or you just want more bells and whistles?

Some Twitter users prefer not to access the service through a browser window, need a few more organizational options than the web page affords, or just want to share Twitter on an external website or blog. You can find plenty of options out there for doing all this and more.

Text messages (SMS delivery)

You can fairly simply opt into receiving Twitter via text messages (SMS delivery). First, you have to set up a mobile device so that Twitter knows where to send your tweets:

1. **From your computer, click the person icon at the top-right of your Twitter home screen and then select the Settings menu.**

   The Settings page opens.

2. **Click the Mobile link.**

3. **Enter your mobile phone number in the text field and then click the Activate Phone button.**

   You're given an alphabetical code and instructed to text this code from your phone to 40404.

4. **Send the the suggested text message from your cellphone to Twitter at 40404.**

This activates the phone and associates it with this Twitter account.

5. **Choose to have text-message notifications on or off, direct messages only, mentions, and replies.**

Make sure that your cellphone carrier has an unlimited text-messaging plan — or that you're willing to pay for a lot of extra texts — before setting Twitter device notifications to On. Twitter doesn't charge for texts, but your carrier might! Laura has unlimited texting even though she doesn't receive any text updates from Twitter, because she loves to use the text commands to add people, send tweets, and send direct messages.

You don't automatically receive device updates from everyone you follow on Twitter. You have to manually turn these device updates on for each individual. To check and see whether any given individual is set to device updates ON or OFF:

1. **Go to that user's profile on Twitter.**

You can access a user's profile by clicking the user's avatar, name, or @username in one of his tweets, and then clicking it again in the pop-up window.

2. **Click their person icon and turn mobile notifications on or off for that person or account.**

Of course, you can also control this setting using SMS on your phone. Send an **ON username** message to turn Device updates on and **OFF username** message to turn off updates.

If you forget who you've set to receive mobile device updates from, you can always go to the list of people you're following by clicking Following to find that information. Click their person icon on the right side of their listing to access the submenu.

Desktop clients

You can access Twitter through one of the many downloadable desktop applications that third-party developers have created using Twitter's API. Some of the most popular applications are Twhirl, Twitterrific, and TweetDeck (shown in Figure 3-11).

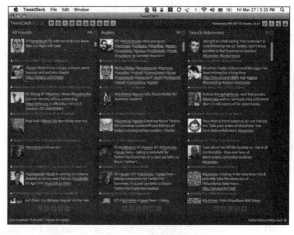

Figure 3-11: Get your Twitter info via TweetDeck.

Basically, a Twitter client allows you to use Twitter from your desktop without having a browser open.

Many of these clients also offer features that Twitter doesn't, including the ability to thread tweets and track conversations, create groups, filter content, open simultaneous accounts, delete direct messages, and more.

These services work by talking to Twitter to get the information they need. So, they don't work if Twitter isn't working; they rely on it to gather and relay the data you see and use.

Echofon

A third-party application created for Twitter is Echofon (www.echofon.com/twitter/firefox), which is a plug-in that you can use with the Mozilla Firefox web browser. In this case, *plug-in* just means that the application gets installed right into the browser and runs from there. It won't run on Safari or Internet Explorer, and you can't use it if you don't use Firefox.

Although most plug-ins and add-ons made for Twitter are safe to put on your computer, always be careful any time you install something new. A good way to tell whether an application is okay is to ask your friends on Twitter whether they use it. Most active Twitter users are happy to provide tips and recommendations.

Mozilla approves plug-ins that have been submitted to its developer program. Plug-ins that are proven not to be harmful are endorsed by Mozilla.

Widgets and gadgets

Twitter and other sites offer widgets (or, as Google calls them, "gadgets") that let you embed information from a service such as Twitter onto other sites so that you can share Twitter more easily. Sometimes, widgets come in the form of HTML code that you can copy and paste into a MySpace profile or blog template. Other times, they come in the form of an application that you have to install on a social-network platform, such as Facebook. You can use dozens and dozens of official and unofficial widgets for Twitter. Using free widget-building tools, anyone can build a widget using any RSS feed as the content supply, so there's no telling how many thousands of Twitter widgets actually exist.

Twitter has an official page where you can find the code for an embeddable widget, complete with step-by-step instructions for installing it. Just go to `http://twitter.com/goodies/widgets`.

You can find an official Twitter application for Facebook, too, which means that you can make your Twitter updates show up as your Facebook status updates, or you can display a badge of your tweets on your Facebook profile. You can find the Twitter application for Facebook at `http://apps.facebook.com/twitter`.

Preview: @Anywhere

At the 2010 South by Southwest Interactive festival, Evan Williams (`@ev`) announced the creation of a new Tweeting platform called @Anywhere. The idea is to re-create the experience of communicating with Twitter users on Twitter.com, but within the context of another website, article, or event.

For example, Twitter users could live-discuss the latest headlines on *The New York Times* (`www.nytimes.com`) or products they're considering purchasing on eBay (`www.ebay.com`).

If you're a site developer, you should visit the @Anywhere development site on Twitter (`dev.twitter.com/docs/anywhere/welcome`) for more details on what @Anywhere is and how to use it. As a consumer, you'll simply run into "Twitter-smart" web pages or apps that will allow you to do things like tweet from that page instead of logging into Twitter using a new window.

Chapter 4

Twitter Minus Twitter.com

• •

• •

*Y*ou can easily get attached to Twitter simply because after you really get started, you're bound to discover many interesting and useful things it can do for you. You can literally take Twitter — and the information, ideas, and friends you connect with on Twitter — everywhere. Mobile applications and text messages give on-the-go users the ability to update their timeline and access their network. E-mail and RSS feeds also allow you to pipe your Twitter stream into your favorite RSS reader or e-mail, or onto your mobile device. Because the Twitter platform is so flexible, you can do almost everything you want with Twitter without needing to visit Twitter.com.

Look around the web, and you'll see that Twitter is a staple on popular social-networking sites and a standard sidebar feature on many blogs. Because of the many ways that users can access and share Twitter on the web, you can discover it in all sorts of useful places, from tweets about specific neighborhoods on RentWiki (www.rentwiki.com) to live widgets on major media sites.

In this chapter, we show you how you can use Twitter without having to browse to Twitter.com. When you realize how you can access Twitter from anywhere, you're bound to discover ways to make it even more useful to you.

Tweeting with Your Cellphone

Many twitterers use the service almost exclusively on their mobile phones. You can use Twitter on your mobile device in three ways:

- ✔ SMS (text messages) to and from 40404 (or your country's short code)
- ✔ Twitter's mobile website (http://m.twitter.com) if you have a web browser on your cellphone
- ✔ Downloadable applications for BlackBerry, Android, Windows Mobile, and iPhone smartphones

Via text messaging

Although text messaging (or SMS) is the most basic way to access Twitter via your cellphone, you want to first make sure that your cellphone plan encompasses unlimited texting. Otherwise, your monthly bill may end up skyrocketing. Check before you enable SMS updates!

After you make sure that you can afford your mobile
texting plan, you can easily use SMS to update Twitter
on the go. (Turn to Chapter 1 for instructions on how to
associate your cellphone with your Twitter account.)

 One caveat: Although the maximum length for a
standard text message is 160 characters, Twitter's
maximum is 140 characters. You have to manually
verify that you aren't going over the Twitter limit
because otherwise, Twitter cuts off your SMS
tweet at 140 characters.

In addition to sending tweets as SMS messages from
your phone, you can receive your contacts' tweets on
your phone via SMS. Setting this up takes a little more
work. First, think long and hard about how noisy you
want your phone to be each day. Most Twitter users
find that they can handle between 10 and 20 peoples'
tweets being sent to their phone before the constant
incoming text stream becomes overwhelming. Luckily,
even power users have discovered that they can take
advantage of SMS tweets to their phone by being really
selective about whose actual tweets they get via SMS.
It's not all-or-nothing.

To receive tweets from your contacts on your
cellphone

1. **Open your Twitter home screen.**

2. **Click the person icon and select Settings.**

3. **On the Settings page, click the Mobile link.**

4. **Find the Device Updates section.**

5. **Set that you want to receive mobile updates
   (Message Notifications).**

   Twitter allows you to take updates on your
   phone, limit notifications to direct messages,

include mentions and replies from people you
follow (or indeed, anyone), or opt-out entirely of
text notifications.

Select the appropriate check boxes to enable
those messages.

6. **Make a list of people whose tweets you really
   want to receive directly as SMS messages on
   your phone.**

   These people can be anyone — friends, family,
   influencers, clients — whatever works for you.

7. **Click Home to return to your Home page.**

8. **List those you follow by clicking the Following
   link, and then click the person icon next to
   their listing.**

9. **Select (toggle on/off) mobile notifications.**

Via smartphones or PDAs

If you have a smartphone, BlackBerry, or PDA with
web capabilities, you can use Twitter's mobile website (http://m.twitter.com), or a number of
other third-party mobile websites like Hahlo
(http://hahlo.com/), pretty much the way you
use Twitter.com on your computer. You can also
download applications that allow you to use Twitter
as an application on your phone. You can find several
popular applications. The following are just a sam-
pling of what's available for various devices:

   ✔ **For iPhone:** Check out Twitter (http://
     itunes.apple.com/us/app/twitter),
     Twittelator (www.stone.com/Twittelator),
     Echofon (www.echofon.com), and Twitterrific
     (http://iconfactory.com/software/
     twitterrific).

✔ **For BlackBerry:** Blackberry has released its own Twitter client, accessible via App World or on the RIM website (http://us.blackberry.com/smartphones/features/social/twitter.jsp?). For other options, try Blackbird (http://dossy.org/twitter/blackbird), Tiny Twitter (http://tinytwitter.com), and OpenBeak (www.orangatame.com/products/openbeak).

✔ **For Android Devices:** Twidroid (http://twidroyd.com) and Seesmic (https://seesmic.com/seesmic-social/mobile) seem to be the favorites.

✔ **For Windows Mobile:** Look into PockeTwit (http://code.google.com/p/pocketwit) and Tiny Twitter (www.tinytwitter.com).

Play around with an application's options a bit until you find one you like best. They're all a little bit different, and they have varying advantages based on how you use Twitter, how often you tweet, how big your network is, and so forth.

Location! Location! Location!

One great advantage to becoming a mobile Twitter user is the ability to live-tweet from wherever you are, on location. Many Twitter clients for mobile — including the mobile.twitter.com site for iPhone — allow for location-based information to be sent along with your tweets.

Each application lets you opt-in to this service, so please check the user guides for each application on how to opt-in.

When you're tweeting your location, you risk making it easy for people to find you or learn where you live. Adding location to your tweets is a fun and useful feature, and although location-based technology isn't pin-point accurate yet, be sure you remember that your digital footprint is telling a story about you and your daily habits! So, just be careful.

Using Twitter through Your E-Mail

When someone new starts following you, Twitter sends you an e-mail that contains a link so that you can check out that user's profile right away to see whether you want to follow him back. These e-mails save quite a bit of time and hassle — you don't have to try to remember who followed you and when.

If you don't have the time or the need to follow back your new followers right away, use whatever options your e-mail client (or web service) provides to search, file, or tag certain messages received. Setting up a mail filter to segment those notifications outside of your normal e-mail inbox can be really useful. Those e-mails then wait for you to process more efficiently in batches when it's convenient for you.

You can also set up your Twitter account so that direct messages are sent to your e-mail inbox:

1. **On your Home page, click the person icon and select Settings.**

2. **On the Settings screen, click the Notifications link.**

3. **Select the check box for any type of the e-mail notification you'd like to receive; clear check boxes to disable those notifications.**

Even if you're receiving direct notifications through Twitter and your mobile phone, you may also want to get them by e-mail. Most modern e-mail applications, including Webmail software, allow you to search through your mail. By always having a copy in your e-mail inbox, you can much more easily retrieve and find a direct message that you receive. Otherwise, there is no way to search your direct messages, which can be a problem.

Although Twitter can send you e-mails, it has no mechanism that allows you to send updates, replies, or direct messages directly via e-mail. Twitter does provide a link in the e-mail that you can click to open pages at Twitter.com (or mobile Twitter), where you can send Twitter info.

To work around this limitation, some developers have used the API to come up with e-mail clients for Twitter, including tweetymail (http://tweety mail.com, shown in Figure 4-1) and Twittermail at TwitterCounter.com (http://twittercounter.com/ pages/twittermail, shown in Figure 4-2). Both of these web apps enable you to interact with users and update Twitter directly from your e-mail address.

As with many third-party web apps, tweetymail and Twittermail ask for your Twitter username and password. If you don't think you can trust a site with your credentials, just don't use it! Luckily, OAuth (Open Authentication) holds the promise of letting you give third-party applications limited permission to function with your account without giving away your password and the ability to access everything about your account.

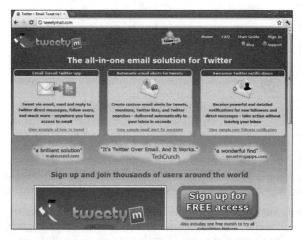

Figure 4-1: tweetymail offers enhanced Twitter notifications and e-mail-based replies.

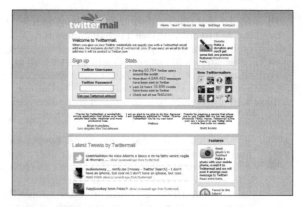

Figure 4-2: Twittermail looks like Twitter, but integrates Twitter with your e-mail inbox.

Swimming Your Stream with RSS Feeds

If you want to keep tabs on your Twitter network without logging into Twitter.com, you can use *RSS* (Really Simple Syndication) to pull in your Twitter stream like it's a blog. Really Simple Syndication is a format for delivering dynamic web content — blogs, news stories, and multimedia — in a standard, easy-to-read format (called *feeds*). RSS isn't a website or a web page: It's a raw data feed for the content on a web page or website. You often find RSS on blogs and news sites, but any site that has live and updating content, including Twitter, can use RSS.

Most modern browsers (such as Safari, Firefox, and later versions of Internet Explorer) have RSS reading capabilities built in, but you likely want to use a dedicated application or website to handle your feeds because then you can go back later and search them, refer to them, catch up on many at once, and more.

An RSS reader, such as NewsGator's NetNewsWire or FeedDemon (www.newsgator.com) or Google Reader (www.google.com/reader), aggregates RSS feeds, which you can then read. Within these applications, you subscribe to an RSS feed, which allows you to access your favorite web content within a single destination and keep up with frequently updated sites.

RSS is a fundamental part of Twitter because it allows users to share and access timelines from virtually anywhere on the web, as well as through desktop applications and mobile devices. Each user's timeline has its own RSS feed, which you can read via an RSS reader.

Grabbing RSS feeds

If you have a smartphone that has RSS capabilities, you can use that smartphone to get Twitter while you're on the go. To grab the RSS feed for your home screen, click the RSS button in the bottom-left of the sidebar and follow the specific instructions for your RSS reader. If you hover over the RSS icon in your browser (depending on which browser you use, the location of this icon varies), it also displays the feed address. You can then add the feed address to your RSS reader of choice, such as Google Reader or Bloglines.

You can obtain an individual RSS feed address for your home screen (the Twitter stream of all your friends), the Everyone page (the public timeline of all Twitter users), and your @*username* page — but not for your Direct Messages page. To read direct messages, you have to rely on e-mail, text messages, or another method.

Also, Twitter Search has RSS capabilities built in. You can pull any search that you perform on Twitter Search into an RSS feed directly from the site.

Sending RSS feeds back to Twitter

Twitterfeed (http://twitterfeed.com) is a third-party application you can use to send RSS feeds to Twitter so that each item in the feed "posts" as a tweet. It turns out you can accomplish a lot by using this application:

✔ **Announce new blog posts.** If you have a blog and want to promote each new post by using your Twitter account, you can have Twitterfeed pull in the RSS of your blog and send the title of the post and a link to Twitter (posting it as a

tweet from your account). You may find this feature particularly useful if you update your blog
frequently.

✔ **Create and share a *link blog*.** At Pistachio
Consulting, we maintain a link blog of some of
the best articles we can find about the business
use of Twitter. We use www.delicious.com/
touchbaseblog to track, tag, and share these
articles, and we direct the RSS for that Delicious
account to @touchbase on Twitter (along with
a feed to our http://www.touchbaseblog.
com posts, too). That way, business users of
Twitter can easily access up-to-date case stud-
ies, articles, best practices, and ideas simply by
following a Twitter stream.

✔ **Re-tweet hashtags.** If you're running an event
and want everyone who plans to attend that
event to be able to send a message to everyone
else, search that hashtag on http://search.
twitter.com and then grab the RSS feed from
the Twitter search results page and feed it into
the event's account. Now everyone at the event
can follow your single event account to see all
the hashtagged tweets being shared. *Note:* This
will work for any search term. Be creative!

✔ **Translate tweets automatically.** This one is
advanced, but if you want to reach an interna-
tional audience by sending your tweets in
another language and you're comfortable play-
ing with advanced tools like Yahoo! Pipes
(http://pipes.yahoo.com/pipes), you can
actually pull in a Twitter stream, automatically
translate it into a number of different languages,
and then publish the stream to its own language-
specific Twitter account by using Twitterfeed.
Just be sure to mention on that account bio that
it's automated, or native speakers will wonder
why the writing is so awkward!

Limit the number of times that you have to feed send messages to Twitter so that you don't send too many tweets and irritate your followers. You should also mention in the bio for the account if it is heavily — or completely — automated.

Chapter 5

Establishing Your Twitter Voice

. . . .

In This Chapter

▶ Diving into Twitter

▶ Deciding whether to tweet for work or fun

▶ Figuring out whom you're tweeting to

▶ Being yourself on Twitter

▶ Knowing what to keep personal and private

. . . .

*I*f you let it, Twitter can conveniently become an integral part of your day-to-day life. Twitter is available almost everywhere — you can update your Twitter feed many ways on many platforms. Wherever you have Internet or cellular coverage, you can more or less use Twitter. The mechanics are pretty easy.

But as you get up to speed and even "embrace the twecosystem," writing and sharing in only 140 characters at a time definitely takes some getting used to. It may seem a bit limiting at first, but over time that limitation changes the way you write and communicate. If you plan to use the service with some regularity, you'll probably want to think at least a little bit about how your updates compare with the image you want to convey.

In this chapter, we explore different approaches to using Twitter and how you can find your own unique voice.

Business or Pleasure?

When you first sign up for a Twitter account, you don't follow anyone yet, and nobody follows you. Updating your feed may seem a bit awkward. You're tweeting into the void, you have no idea who's really listening (if anyone), and you're almost certainly wondering what the heck the point of tweeting even is. Don't feel bad — most everyone's first tweet (see Figure 5-1) is a little awkward. But if you follow our advice, you should be able to get the hang of Twitter in no time!

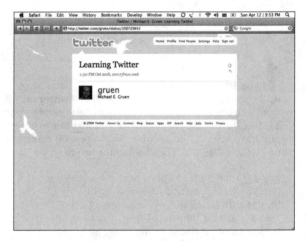

Figure 5-1: An example first tweet.

When you start following users and other users start following you, you may want to think about what sort of things you want to share with your following. For many new users, one of the great debates is whether to use Twitter for business or pleasure, and we address that a lot in this chapter. You might have joined Twitter for either reason (or both). As you come to embrace the medium to its fullest, you will find yourself figuring out what kind of voice you want to use on Twitter. The answer, as with so many answers about Twitter, depends entirely on what you want to get out of the Twitter experience.

Part of determining your identity on Twitter involves choosing your username (which we cover in Chapter 1). If you choose a nickname or pseudonym for your username, you probably aim for Twitter personal use. If you use your business name as your Twitter handle, you likely intend to create a presence for your company. But if you use your real name as your username (which is probably the best way to go), it simply implies that you are who you say you are — and you can take your account in the direction that makes the most sense to you as you evolve. That's one reason why you probably want to use your real name or some variation of it.

Whatever name you pick, you can change it at any time on your Twitter account's Settings page. (Look for Username, in the Account section.)

No matter what you name your Twitter presence, you need a voice and personality that's uniquely yours. We go over some tips and thoughts on how to make your Twitter voice your own in the section "You as you on Twitter," later in this chapter.

Your business on Twitter

Can you use something as simple as Twitter for business? Absolutely! However, you can't exactly adopt a salesperson "Sell! Sell! Sell!" mentality on Twitter. To operate as a successful business presence on Twitter, you need to

- ✔ Master the art of give and take.
- ✔ Figure out how to engage your Twitter base in conversation.
- ✔ Give your audience, clients, and customers a reason to read your tweets.

Twitter is a conversational medium. For businesses to mesh well with user expectations, companies and businesses need to understand how to navigate the landscape as a brand.

If you're representing a large company (such as @JetBlue or @Starbucks), your Twitter presence might be a little more complicated because you're not representing just yourself, but your business — and for some companies, that may mean tens of thousands of people. That's a lot of responsibility!

If you're managing a Twitter presence on behalf of your company, we highly encourage you to start a separate account for yourself so that you can get used to the service. Before you start tweeting on behalf of your business, know what users expect from brands and businesses, and how customers like to be approached. Getting used to how businesses operate on Twitter can prevent you from making a serious faux pas down the road. That said, a lot of what makes the best business accounts great is their personality and humanity, so the case can also be made not to always have two different (business and personal) accounts.

You as you on Twitter

Although Twitter can be a powerful tool for business owners and employees, it's just as powerful for individuals who really have no intention of conducting any sort of business on it (although business might happen accidentally).

Twitter was originally popular helping individuals keep in touch with their friends and acquaintances via mini-updates. Many personal Twitterers still tend to use Twitter in this manner, updating a close circle of friends about thoughts and happenings in their lives. Over time, you can keep up with — and even make new — friends you might otherwise not contact often. Twitter removes many communication barriers.

A few things to consider for your personal Twitter presence:

✔ **Keeping your tweets private:** If it helps you feel more comfortable with your personal use of Twitter, you can set your updates to Private. Enabling the privacy feature ensures that no one, other than the users you authorize, has access to your updates. Note: If your friends choose to retweet something pithy you said, that tweet they share from you isn't private. However, setting your updates to Private also prevents Twitter Search from picking up your tweets; it's a minor inconvenience that you may be willing to accept if you really feel strongly about protecting your personal updates from the world.

✔ **Introducing your business:** Regardless of whether you plan to build your business by using Twitter "just as a person," you might want to include some information about your occupation and company in your Twitter profile, and perhaps add a link back to your company's online presence. The *social capital* (trust, thought leadership, and more) that you earn within the Twitter community may lead to new opportunities for you and for your business. Also, your opinions and statements may be biased because of your job, so in the interests of transparency, disclosure is a good idea.

✔ **Making it personal:** You don't have to include any business information on Twitter if you don't want to. Twitter was built with personal connections in mind. Twitter is personal, so dress up your profile and adjust your settings in a way that makes sense to you and what you want to get out of your Twitter experience.

If you're twittering as an individual who works at a company, use a real photo of yourself as your avatar and put your company logo on the Twitter background that you use for your page. By using this setup, you let people know that you're affiliated with the company, but users don't mistake you for the company's official twitterer. Be sure you follow your company's regulations regarding what you're allowed to share. For example, many Apple employees can't reveal that they work for the company.

Mixing business with pleasure

Some of the most successful Twitter personalities have embraced Twitter by transparently sharing personal, professional, family, and other aspects of themselves all rolled together. This is nothing wildly new. We've always spent time with colleagues, clients, and our professional network at the golf course, out to dinner, attending charity events, and the like. Most networking events have a highly social component to them. It's simple: People like to do business with people they like.

Some find balancing your personal life and your professional life on Twitter tricky at first, but you can definitely do it. Give yourself time to discover what you're comfortable doing. We don't really know anyone who completely stops talking about work when out with friends — or vice versa — because work (whether we like it or not) is a big part of who we all are. Because Twitter is built for human communications, it can handle many facets of your life; you just have to find your own balance.

It's all about balance

Balance is important on Twitter, as in life, if you want to connect with people in a genuine, mutually beneficial way. Twitter is pretty much of a "what you give is what you get" kind of place. Your true voice is often the best bet, unless you're really constrained for business reasons and need to rein it in. Accounts that are nothing but business (or worse, strictly business-promotional) all the time may have a pretty hard time growing much of an engaged base.

Want to be uber-personal all the time? There is absolutely nothing wrong with that, but it will influence the size and shape of your network. Don't be offended if it's not everybody's cup of tea. Present yourself the way you feel most comfortable.

If you cover both business and personal stuff on your account but aren't an official "for the business" twitterer, it can be good to go easy on how frequently you tweet about business-only stuff. We get asked for a specific ratio all the time, and it's really hard to say. As car ads say, "Your mileage will vary." (On Twitter, that would read, #ymwv.) Try a mix that's comfortable to you and then just see whether you're getting the results you hoped for. Also, please remember, the number of followers is much less important than the quality of the conversations. For long-term sustainable value, true engagement beats tonnage any day.

If you're updating under your business handle (for us, it's @dummies), followers probably expect that nearly all tweets from that account will relate to that business. After all, they're following that account for business info! If you're really inconsistent, off-topic, or overboard personally all the time, and violate your followers' expectations too much, you may find your audience shrinking. Everyone needs to strike a balance, but most successful brand accounts stay relatively on topic. If you're an individual twitterer, followers probably want to hear about you and how you're going about your business. It's a subtle difference but an important point to establish yourself as genuine, and not a selfish peddler of goods.

Your goal should be to permit your followers to get a good understanding of what your business offers and come to trust you as who you are. Make the bulk of the content that you add to Twitter about you and the value that you provide (as a person and through your work). Think of some updates as "give" and other updates as "take": When you share or talk about things that are genuinely useful and helpful to customers, you're providing something they want. That sets the stage for occasionally promoting the goods or services that you sell, because you've earned the trust and attention of your readers. Just remember that promotional tweets that aren't framed from the perspective of your customer's needs too often come across as a "take" because you're asking for followers to buy what you're selling.

Want to know if the balance you strike is effective? Re-read your tweets at the end of the day or the end of the week and keep an eye on replies, re-tweets, the numbers of people clicking links you share, and, yes, follower growth. If you feel that your update stream comes off as too sales-y, then back off on the selling and stick to providing value. Twitter's about being a genuine individual. Over time, Twitter gives your followers a lot of information about you, who you are and what you represent. That builds trust, confidence, and interest in you. Be real.

Be yourself

 Like with the individual and business-only accounts, be sure to give your name in your bio. Transparency about who you are and what you do can go a long way toward growing your Twitter foundation. And a good Twitter foundation is key to establishing a stable and growing Twitter network. Using your real name adds to your value as an individual.

Just as in other business interactions, you need to be genuine on Twitter and establish yourself as a trustworthy, multidimensional person.

At the same time, think carefully about how much of your private matters you want to share. Occasional

mention of your love life, health, and other more personal stuff can be very funny, very humanizing, and
very honest, but being really negative, self-indulgent,
or tedious about the same will put people off. When
you really need to talk about those things, it's very
possible you'll find supportive people on Twitter.
Having found something in common or someone who
wants to help, you may even get into a more in-depth
conversation with a twitterer via direct message (DM)
or leave Twitter altogether via e-mail, IM, or over your
favorite beverage. You can also definitely connect
with people on more public personal topics like
sports, TV, books, movies, or politics without reveal-
ing all your deepest secrets.

As a person on Twitter, you might find value in
talking about your business problems in the
open. Many fellow twitterers are willing to give
you advice about how to overcome a business
challenge or situation. If you've spent time culti-
vating a network that works for you, you have
many resources at your fingertips. Ask them!

Identifying Your Audience

Whether you're a business or an individual on
Twitter, if you want to grow your Twitter network, it's
helpful to think about your audience. If you haven't
transplanted your existing social networks onto
Twitter, it may be a good time to do that and to put a
bit of time and effort into expanding your network.

Think about the kinds of people you'd like to talk to
or the subjects you'd like to discuss through Twitter.
Trying to build up business? Target your customers.
Want to communicate with other avid cyclists on

Twitter? Search keywords and look to see who tweets about major cycling events. Send updates that are relevant to whomever you'd like to reach or about the topics that interest you and engage yourself in that conversation. Yes, it's that easy.

When you start using Twitter, it's pretty hard to determine who your audience will be — your followers grow based on what value you can provide for other users. So, if you're trying to reach other cyclists to talk about racing, the Tour de France, or the latest in derailleur technology, start talking about it and search for other users already chatting about the subject. (You can find out about searching for users and topics in Chapters 1 and 2.)

 You don't have to be one-dimensional in your Twitter chat. For example, if you want to engage cyclists, you don't always and only have to talk about cycling. People understand that you have more to you than a single activity or idea (unless you're a company or targeted Twitter account, for which the implicit rules are a little different — see "Your business on Twitter," earlier in this chapter), so don't feel that you need to talk about only one thing to be of value to your target audience. Be yourself and talk about the things you like; but, if you want to engage other cyclists, just talk a bit more about cycling than anything else. That's all. Over time, your cycling network will grow.

Viewing your network

Although you have little direct control over who follows you (however you can block people you don't want to be associated with), you can easily see what sort of user you're attracting. Browse through your list of Followers and click through to open some of their profiles to get a general idea of who's following you (on any Twitter screen, click the Followers link under your name in the sidebar).

When you look into who's following you, you might realize that you're drawing unexpected people as followers. Reaching people and businesses you never expected to reach is most likely not a bad thing. If you're a business, unpredicted followers could show that you're increasing your business's social reach, meaning a sign of successful Twitter use. If you're twittering as an individual, you're broadening your horizons — and other users consider you and your tweets interesting.

Diversifying your network

You can help guide who tends to follow you by talking about a myriad of topics. People aren't one-dimensional, and no one really expects you to be on-point all the time. Although you may have interests that you talk about more than others, getting a sense of what you're talking about and whom you're talking to can come in handy — it enables you to target your tweets to topics that are most interesting to your followers.

One of our favorite tools for understanding how often and what you're updating is TweetStats (www.tweet stats.com). This tool enables you to see who you're talking to, when you're talking, and what you're talking about — all in graph form. Figure 5-2 shows an example of the type of information TweetStats reports.

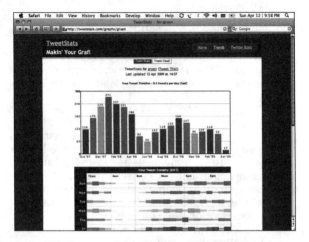

Figure 5-2: You can see a graph of your tweet density.

Targeting specific networks

If you're targeting specific people with whom you want to interact more regularly, find a way to add value to the interactions for them. You can target these types of people by searching keywords and hashtags for that topic and seeing who uses them and who the real leaders appear to be. When you're following a few key people within that interest area, look for whom they talk to, listen to, and value. For example, if you're a gardener, check to see who Martha Stewart (@MarthaStewart) follows and talks to about gardening topics. Click through any appealing @replies and consider following those people. You can also use this information to get a sense of what's important to any given twitterer and what types of information they like to receive. With Twitter, you can essentially browse not only the connections between people, but also between topics of interest. You can also easily drop into active ongoing conversations about specific themes. One or two key people can lead you to an entire subject matter landscape on Twitter.

In a very real sense, an individual or Twitter account that represents something can become the foundation for a community. Likewise, if you're trying to target a specific type of individual, go to the Twitter streams of those individuals and see what they're tweeting about. Join the conversation that they're having with other people and engage those other people, as well. Over time, if you're adding value to that conversation, then other people look to you as a person who's involved and relevant in that community, whether it's computer programming, baking cupcakes, or cancer research.

Measuring influence

While you start to gain a foothold within communities on Twitter, you might want to get a sense of what your network looks like and how far your updates travel.

As you read, please bear in mind that some of the less measurable results are the most important. The most important thing to measure is the thing you're actually trying to accomplish, not just numbers for numbers' sake. Are you meeting new friends? Finding new business leads? Sharing information widely about issues important to you?

Do your messages spread? Messages can be much more important influencers within Twitter than influential accounts and individuals, because good messages get repeated. A truly great message, even if it starts in quiet little corners of Twitter among people with small following networks, will echo and get repeated until eventually it reaches much of the network.

Twitter itself has a very primitive way of measuring your reach: You have following and followers counts. Although those numbers would seem to provide a good baseline for understanding how far your updates go and to whom, they don't say much about what types of people follow you and how influential those followers are. In response, the Twitter community has developed a number of tools to help gauge and measure influence and reach. Less ethical people aggressively boost their follower numbers, sometimes through questionable habits like following people just until they follow back and then dropping them to go follow someone else. Important lessons? Don't automatically trust an account with a really high number of followers. Don't build your network around high numbers at the cost of high relevance and high engagement.

TwitterGrader (`http://tweet.grader.com`), shown in Figure 5-3, can help you figure out how you compare with other users, even if they use fairly arbitrary measures.

For all intents and purposes, these numbers don't really measure influence or reach. The results you can get from these sites are so imprecise and subjective that they provide only a rough understanding of how influence flows through the Twitter ecosystem. First and foremost, use Twitter to communicate; and, although high follower counts may indicate genuine popularity, they can be gamed and don't necessarily indicate importance or quality.

Figure 5-3: TwitterGrader, suggesting the humble @pistachio's visibility.

Understanding your extended network

Twitter, by itself, can tell you only the number of people you follow and the number of people who follow you. As described in the previous section, those numbers give you just part of the story.

If 100 people follow you and communicate with you, then your actual extended network is much larger than 100 people because conversations relay messages and connect new people on Twitter. Say that Follower #86 has 1,000 followers. Whenever Follower #86 mentions your name, 1,000 people receive an update that contains your name. And you may find that kind of exposure quite useful. Twitter is an excellent way to "harness the power of loose ties" or benefit from friends of friends of friends who are more likely to know about things nobody in your social group knows.

If Boston-based Laura was trying to locate a venue in Nashville, Tennessee, to hold a Twitter marketing seminar, she might send an update that reads, "Trying to locate a good 700-person venue in Nashville to give a talk. A place to stay would be nice, too. Suggestions?" Because thousands of people read Laura's Twitter stream, chances are good someone lives in Nashville. If any of those handful wanted to connect Laura with a local business owner, they might ask their own networks, who may have an answer based on their own geography. In this sense, Laura's primary network gives her secondary access to all her follower's networks, as well.

It's pretty cool how friends of friends can end up becoming your direct friends, too. Say you're following five friends, and two of them are constantly communicating (via `@replies`) with some other person whom you don't know. Out of curiosity, you may start following that other person just to make sense of your friends' conversations. Because you're friends with two people that the other person talks to frequently, he follows you back. Now, all of a sudden, you have both a larger Twitter network and an extended network.

Keeping Your Tweets Authentic

Because of the frequency and personal nature of what people share on Twitter, any twitterer absolutely must be genuine and real, whether she's representing a business or tweeting as an individual. Joining

Twitter as a private citizen is the route many users take, even if they have business to promote. Twitter is ideally suited for personal connection, and you can often more easily make yourself accessible and personable when you use Twitter as a person, not as your business.

Joining the conversation

You see the phrase "join the conversation" bandied about a lot on Twitter. If you're representing a business, you can get a dialog going very easily: Just search for users who have mentioned your products or the types of problems you solve and follow them. If you have something relevant to say, engage them in conversation using the mention they made as a starting point.

If you're representing a business, mentioning little-known facts or interesting things about what you do or sell can start a conversation. You can also talk about your staff; tell interested twitterers how you (or someone else) make what you sell; or take the easiest route of all and ask your fellow Twitter users what they think of your product or service, and how they think you can improve or expand.

Sharing links

By way of getting started, many new users start sharing links with a bit of commentary on their Twitter stream, as shown in Figure 5-4. For many users, sending a link provides a great way to get a commentary started about something you find interesting. Give it a shot and see what happens. Here are the basics for sharing links.

Figure 5-4: This update comments on a link and includes that link.

1. **Copy the link's URL and paste it in the Compose New Tweet field.**

2. **Type a comment about the link in the same field (before or after the link).**

3. **Post your tweet by clicking the Tweet button.**

   Usually after you post the tweet, Twitter shortens the URL for you using its link-truncation service, t.co.

Some users post a lot of links, and some users like to use RSS or other tools to automatically update their Twitter streams with links to interesting articles that they're reading. Others just post links by hand.

Linking to interesting articles changes how your Twitter audience perceives you. People follow you because you add value to their Twitter streams; but if you flood your stream with links that aren't relevant to your audience, you may start to annoy some of your following. By adding a link to a tweet that you post, you draw attention to the targeted web page, photo, or video, and you're implicitly endorsing it as a good use of your followers' time. Abusing that assumption will erode the interest and trust your followers have in you and reduce the effectiveness of your network.

Image is everything

Your update stream is by far the most important part of your Twitter profile. However, your profile's presentation also needs to reflect something about you. In the same way that you wear a nice set of clothes to a job interview, you want to dress up your profile so that it reflects the image that you want to convey to the world.

Although you may have your update stream protected in your Twitter account's settings, anyone in the world can view your Twitter profile (at `http://twitter.com/yourusername`). Be sure that you're comfortable with the world seeing whatever you put in your profile.

Whether you're a business or a private citizen, your followers and potential followers react much more favorably if you include in your Twitter profile a photo of yourself and a link to something about you. People like to know who they're talking to, and when you present an image that reflects who you are, other people become willing to be honest and open with you.

If you're representing a large, iconic brand on Twitter, you can set your Twitter profile in your corporate colors. However, because Twitter's strength is in personal connections, you need to have actual people representing your brand's Twitter presence. Use a service such as CoTweet (http://cotweet.com), shown in Figure 5-5, to mark each tweet with its author, and in the 160-character bio on Twitter.com, let readers know who each set of initials belongs to.

Too many team members to list? You can show them off in your background graphic the way @CoTweet itself does.

Figure 5-5: You can "sign" Tweets by author by using co-tags in CoTweet.

Being genuine

Authentic people and businesses, using Twitter in a real and interactive way, can experience tremendous growth and return on investment from Twitter because they make real contributions and build up a rich base of trust, influence, and social capital. People respond much better to an authentic, human voice. They engage more closely because they feel comfortable responding, retweeting, and otherwise paying attention to the genuine voice. Bring some value to the twitterverse by adding your authentic contributions, whatever those may be.

For example, if you're tweeting about politics, whether you're a conservative, moderate, liberal, apathetic, or whatever, feel free to agree or disagree with someone — Twitter is, after all, a digital extension of real life, so if you want to engage in that type of dialog, be yourself. Don't try to come off as something you're not just to appeal to people.

If you're representing a business or tweeting on behalf of your company, you probably want to avoid politics, religion, sex, and other hot-button topics, so as not to offend your potential customers.

Your update stream speaks volumes about you. Twitter is a network built on trust and relationships, and being insincere jeopardizes the quality and effectiveness of your network, both on- and offline. You lose some of that hard-won trust that you've been building since you joined Twitter.

Even though you want to be genuine and real at all times, remember that you can easily forget to be nice to people behind the safety of a monitor and keyboard thousands of miles away. Treat others with respect, as you hope to be treated, and you can have a positive online experience. Try not to engage in arguments over petty things — this behavior gets you branded as a troll, and people start to avoid you and stop taking you seriously.

Evangelizing your causes

When you're on Twitter as an individual, if you share
a favorite cause or a local event in a way that makes it
interesting to others, you'll attract those with common
interests. They may get involved and show support,
and the more fellow twitterers know about you and
about the things you have in common, the more connections and ideas will flow in your network.

Don't be afraid to voice your support for social
causes and charities. By tweeting about your cause,
you both spread awareness about what's important
to you (which may lead to more contributions for that
cause or charity) and give your audience a better idea
of who you are as a person.

So, if you're passionate about cancer research,
domestic violence, or another cause and want to have
a fundraiser for it, a Twitter update that you send
about the fundraiser might get repeated and reach
50, 500, 5,000, or 50,000 people (or more) who are
directly and indirectly connected to you. Spread
the love!

Many have raised money for worthy causes right on
Twitter. One of the first was Beth Kanter (@kanter),
whose network sent a Cambodian woman to college
in a matter of a few hours of Twitter conversation
about it and links to a donation site.

Keeping Twitter Personal . . . but Not Too Personal

Above all else, remember that Twitter is a public
forum. Even when you're talking to your trusted
Twitter network, your tweets are very much public;

Google and other search engines still index them, and anyone on the web can link to them.

You can adjust your settings to prevent search engines and the occasional passerby from viewing your updates by protecting your account.

All the public exposure that Twitter offers can really help promote you and your business, but that exposure also comes with some responsibilities:

✔ **Use common sense!** Don't publicly tweet or @reply someone your address, phone number, or other personal details that you should keep private. Send that kind of information via DM — or, even better, via e-mail, instant message, or phone. Keeping your personal details private protects both you and anyone in your care, such as your kids.

✔ **Use DMs cautiously.** Typing **d** *username* and then your message does send a private direct message from any Twitter interface. But trust us, if you made a typo or wrote **dm** *username,* you would not be the first person to accidentally post a private DM publicly. In fact, the problem was so rampant that you can use the dm shortcode to DM someone. But, in our opinion, that doubles your chances for a typo, so keep in the habit of using just d.

To avoid accidental updates, make it a habit to view your follower's page, click the person icon (not yours, which stays at the top of the screen), and then choose Send a Direct Message. Better yet, use an even more secure medium like e-mail or even encryption. *Never* send passwords, credit card numbers, Social Security numbers, or other valuable private data by Twitter (or even e-mail).

> ✔ **Maintain boundaries.** Try to be aware of how
> you are (or aren't) maintaining boundaries with
> the people you interact with frequently on
> Twitter. Especially before you agree to meet
> someone in person, take a look at how you've
> interacted in the past and make sure that you've
> kept your relationship clear from the start,
> whether it's for business or friendship.

Protecting personal details

Many people opt to not even use the real names of
family members or children who don't use Twitter.
Twitterers commonly refer to relatives, friends, and
kids by nicknames or initials, just to give those loved
ones a layer of protection. Use a bit of caution and ask
permission before tweeting someone's real name (or
any other information that we mention). Laura, for
example, uses her daughters' initials S and Z, as shown
in Figure 5-6. Twitter is a powerful influence on search
engines, so casual mentions of unique names remain
findable for a long time. If Laura even used their first
names on her tweets (which all also contain her last
name), they'd likely appear visibly in Google search
results for their firstname lastname. Don't believe her?
A Google search for Z Fitton (or Z Fitton Pistachio)
brings up a few recent tweets about her antics.

The same words of caution go for any number of personal details. Dive into information about your health
or your private life in private conversation. Although
being authentic and a little bit personal goes a long
way on Twitter, everyone understands that you need
a layer of privacy to keep you, your loved ones, and
the details about them safe.

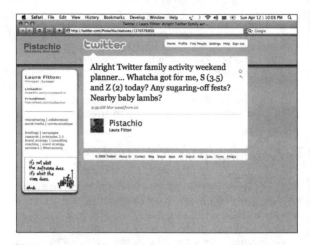

Figure 5-6: Laura (@pistachio) referencing her children in a tweet.

Maximizing privacy and safety

After you use Twitter for a while, you've given away a lot of information about yourself. If you mention who you spend time with or that you always hang out at a certain cafe, someone can start tracking where you've been and what you're doing. We don't want to scare you, but whenever you post in a public medium, anyone could go through the information you've published, later on, and start piecing things together. Laura loves the unique charms of her neighborhood and street, but she keeps the details really fuzzy, preferring Boston as specific enough.

Chapter 6

Ten Useful Twitter-Based Services

....

In This Chapter

▶ Staying in touch with the world through Twitter services

▶ Organizing your Twitter life

▶ Keeping up with the folks on Twitter

....

*W*ith events like the Royal Wedding and the earthquake in Japan, and big-name celebrities with a presence on Twitter, buzz about the service has made Twitter go mainstream extremely fast. Because of that, many businesses, causes, and people are creating Twitter-based presences, and hundreds of innovative Twitter-based services are emerging to support that. Some have separate websites, and some you just use directly through Twitter. In no particular order, here are ten that stand out because of their usefulness and overall appeal to Twitter audiences.

BreakingNews

`@BreakingNews http://www.bnonews.com`

Type: News. This simple feed gives you ongoing breaking news from around the world. Actual humans maintain and update it, not an automatic RSS feed. It has a good track record of beating many of the major news outlets for breaking news — and it has a good track record for accuracy, as well.

StockTwits

`@StockTwits http://www.stocktwits.com`

Type: Financial. Cofounded by Howard Lindzon, best known for mashing up Wall Street with video podcasting to create the highly successful WallStrip, StockTwits plays off the fact that investors who tweet like to tweet about stocks. StockTwits is essentially a community and social exchange of snippets of conversation about stocks, using Twitter as the conversation medium at its core. You can use StockTwits at its website, by following @stocktwits, or by using the TweetDeck plug-in.

Tweecious: Use Delicious to Organize the Links You Tweet

`http://friedcell.net/tweecious/get`

Type: Publishing. If you post links to Delicious (`http://delicious.com`; a social bookmarking service that allows you to share links with your friends), this little tool makes it easy for you. Now, your posts to Twitter that include links can also automagically go to Delicious. Tweecious even looks at the rest of the tweet and automatically tags the link with relevant categories or keywords. After you have a Delicious account, Tweecious takes only a moment to set up, and it even reads shortened URLs and extracts the original link.

 People who like to keep track of a variety of web pages and tend to lose them on Twitter may find this tool very handy.

Tweetworks

@Tweetworks

Type: Social threading and conversation tracking. This service, a creation of Mike Langford (@mike langford) helps you track your Twitter use by group or thread, online or on your iPhone with the use of public or private groups.

 Tweetworks allows you to engage in fully threaded conversations, join and create groups on any topic imaginable, and share media with single-click tagging.

ExecTweets

@exectweets http://www.exectweets.com

Type: Networking. Like millions of other people, Laura pretty much laughed at Twitter when she first heard about it. Turns out that's pretty normal. But what made the difference for her was noticing that she could use it to surround herself with successful, interesting people who would motivate her as a homebound working mom.

Nowadays, we have ExecTweets to let you easily follow the tweets of some of the world's smartest, most successful executives. Richard Branson? Check. Jack Welch? Check. Dive in and find inspiration, leadership, ideas, and resources from some of the brightest business minds in the world.

TweetGrid

    www.tweetgrid.com

Type: Search utility. TweetGrid is a powerful Twitter search dashboard that allows you to search for up to nine different topics, events, conversations, hashtags, phrases, people, groups, and so on, in real-time. As new tweets are created, they are automatically updated in the grid with no need to refresh the page.

TweetGrid supports Boolean search operators and other advanced search techniques: for example, using the Boolean operator AND. If two or more words are specified in the search, AND is assumed, meaning that you don't need to type **AND** into the search. The search results will include all of the search terms by default. However, if you wish, you may still type **AND** (in all capital letters) between search terms.

LinkBunch

    http://linkbun.ch

Type: URL shortener. You can use Twitter to link to one URL, but LinkBunch offers a URL shortener for bundles of links. It takes several links and shortens them into one minimal URL that people can click to access the links. When the user clicks the LinkBunch link, he's taken to a page where he sees all the links you bunched together and can click whichever ones he's interested in.

Tweetree

www.tweetree.com

Type: Reading. This little service threads your tweets into a tree, which includes inline links, videos, and other files. If you think the Adobe Air application that you use to view Twitter leaves your stream looking cluttered, or if you have a hard time following conversational "threads" back and forth, Tweetree might be your answer to making your Twitter conversations easier to read.

TwitterGrader

http://tweet.grader.com

Type: Directory. This Twitter-based service ranks you using a secret formula developed by its creators at HubSpot. The system takes into account not only how many followers you have, but how you converse and engage, who follows, talks to, and retweets you, who you follow, and more. Your TwitterGrade of ## is a percentile, claiming that you are more, well, gradeable, than ##% of other twitterers. The service helps you see how you measure up to other tweeters around the web and specifically in your area, and helps you find people whom you may want to follow because they mesh well with your ranking, interests, and location. Ultimately the grade doesn't mean a whole lot, but it will definitely show you who is active in your area.

BLIP.fm

```
http://blip.fm
```

Type: Multimedia sharing. You can use this Twitter-based music service to DJ songs onto Twitter. It has an outstanding database of songs, and the service allows you to make mixes for your Twitter following.